MONEY IN THE BIBLE

Volume 1: Money, Prosperity, and Wealth

BY J. PITTERSON

Published by Celestial Guide Publications

Unless otherwise stated, all scripture quotations are taken from the New King James Version or the King James Version of the Bible.

ISBN 978-1-0688520-2-2 (Paperback)
ISBN 978-1-0688520-3-9 (E-book)
ISBN 978-1-0688520-4-6 (Hardcover)

Copyright © 2024 Celestial Guide Publications
All rights reserved

Table of Contents

Introduction 1

Part 1 – Money in the Bible 5

   Chapter 1 - Money in the Book of Genesis 6
   Chapter 2- Money in the Book of Exodus 16
   Chapter 3 - Money in the Book of Leviticus 23
   Chapter 4 - Money in the Book of Numbers 27
   Chapter 5 - Money in the Book of Deuteronomy 30
   Chapter 6 - Money in the Book of Judges 34
   Chapter 7 - Money in the Books of Kings 37
   Chapter 8 - Money in the Book of 2 Chronicles 44
   Chapter 9 - Money in the Book of Ezra 48
   Chapter 10 - Money in the Book of Nehemiah 50
   Chapter 11 - Money in the Book of Esther 53
   Chapter 12 - Money in the Book of Job 55
   Chapter 13 - Money in the Book of Psalms 57
   Chapter 14 - Money in the Book of Proverbs 59
   Chapter 15 - Money in the Book of Ecclesiastes 61
   Chapter 16 - Money in the Book of Isaiah 63
   Chapter 17 - Money in the Book of Jeremiah 66
   Chapter 18 - Money in the Book of Lamentations 69
   Chapter 19 - Money in the Book of Micah 70
   Chapter 20 - Money in the Book of Matthew 72
   Chapter 21 - Money in the Book of Mark 78
   Chapter 22 - Money in the Book of Luke 80
   Chapter 23 - Money in the Book of John 84
   Chapter 24 - Money in the Book of Acts 85
   Chapter 25 - Money in the Book of 1 Timothy 89

Part 2 – Moneychangers in the Bible 91

   Chapter 26 - Moneychangers in the Book of Matthew 92
   Chapter 27 - Moneychangers in the Book of Mark 93

Part 3 – Prosperity in the Bible 95

   Chapter 28 - Prosperity in the Book of Deuteronomy 96

Chapter 29 - Prosperity in the Book of Samuel 97
Chapter 30 - Prosperity in the Book of 1 Kings 98
Chapter 31 - Prosperity in the Book of Job 101
Chapter 32 - Prosperity in the Book of Psalms 103
Chapter 33 - Prosperity in the Book of Proverbs 107
Chapter 34 - Prosperity in the Book of Ecclesiastes 109
Chapter 35 - Prosperity in the Book of Jeremiah 110
Chapter 36 - Prosperity in the Book of Lamentations 112
Chapter 37 - Prosperity in the Book of Zechariah 113

Part 4 – Wealth in the Bible 115

Chapter 38 - Wealth in the Book of Genesis 116
Chapter 39 - Wealth in the Book of Deuteronomy 117
Chapter 40 - Wealth in the Book of Ruth 119
Chapter 41 - Wealth in the Book of 1 Samuel 120
Chapter 42 - Wealth in the Book of 2 Kings 122
Chapter 43 - Wealth in the Book of 2 Chronicles 123
Chapter 44 - Wealth in the Book of Ezra 125
Chapter 45 - Wealth in the Book of Esther 127
Chapter 46 - Wealth in the Book of Job 128
Chapter 47 - Wealth in the Book of Psalms 130
Chapter 48 - Wealth in the Book of Proverbs 133
Chapter 49 - Wealth in the Book of Ecclesiastes 137
Chapter 50 - Wealth in the Book of Zechariah 139
Chapter 51 - Wealth in the Book of Acts 141
Chapter 52 - Wealth in the Book of 1 Corinthians 143

Part 5 – Wealthy in the Bible 145

Chapter 53 - Wealthy in the Book of Psalms 146
Chapter 54 - Wealthy in the Book of Jeremiah 147

Conclusion 149

Introduction

We are in a time where the gospel, the good news of Jesus Christ, is presented differently than in ancient times. This is because the revelation of God's Word is constantly being renewed. Understanding this allowed the apostle Peter, in 2 Peter 1 verse 12, to introduce the concept of present truth. For it is known that the younger the brain, the less it is able to assimilate complex things. This is why, although the expressions 1+2, a+b and f(x)+g(x) are all additions, they will only be introduced to students at specific times in their mathematics curriculum. Similarly, when one student says that 1-2 = impossible, and another says that 1-2 = -1, they will both be right. For each student approaches the question according to what he has assimilated in his mathematics course because of the level of development of his brain. This is the case for spiritual development. This is why the Scriptures exhort us to remain constantly in the study of the Bible (Joshua 1:8, Psalms 119:130). This renewal in the preaching of the gospel results from a deep understanding of the Scriptures and provokes reactions that are sometimes positive, sometimes negative, and calls for support resources based on the Scriptures. This word of God to Hosea, "My people are destroyed for lack of knowledge" (Hosea 4:6), must be considered a warning not to accept living in ignorance. As part of the writing of this book, our research allowed us to list more than one thousand four hundred (1400) Bible verses related to money, that is to say, more than 4 percent of all the verses in the Bible. What makes money is one of the main themes of this book. From Genesis to Revelation, it is presented in the following forms: money or exchange currencies, real estate, the quantity of livestock, the volume of agricultural production, abundance, the extent of his kingdom or the splendor of his house, precious stones (gold, silver, diamonds, ivory, etc.). God, who does not recognize any other god outside of himself, openly declares that Mammon, the god of money, is a master like Him, and he is the only one He recognizes as his competitor according to Matthew 6:24, where Jesus said: "No one can serve two masters; for either he will hate the one and love the other, or else he will be loyal to the one and despise the other. You cannot serve God and Mammon."

Paradoxically, God uses money and the influence it provides. Let us recall that Jesus paid his taxes and that the influence of money allowed Joseph of Arimathea, in a context where the disciples were hiding for fear of their lives, to recover the body of Jesus from King Herod in order to give him a decent burial. Moreover, He even gave a lot of it to Abraham, Isaac, Jacob, Joseph, Job, David, Solomon, Joseph of Arimathea... and gives it in this era still to his sons: Kenneth E. Hagin, Oral Roberts, Kenneth Copeland, Benny Hinn, Dr Mike Murdock, Chris Oyakhilome, Uebert Angel, David Oyedepo, E.A. Adeboye, Duncan Williams, and many others.

Some people like to say, and even teach, that Jesus was poor. Know that, among his twelve disciples, Jesus had two clearly identified accountants (Judas and Matthew), one of whom played the role of treasurer (Judas). If Jesus was poor, why did he need a treasurer who accompanied him everywhere he went? The multiplication of the loaves in the desert (Mark 6:37) shows us that the disciples had in their small cash box at least the equivalent of a year's salary for a worker. In the Bible, money is presented as a shield, a protective hedge, a strong city, or a blessing ... to name just a few. It amplifies out loud what we say in a low voice or manifests in broad daylight the person we are in private. Money brings respect, trust, influence, power, and access. Money answers everything, as Solomon said. Or as Dr. Mike Murdock so aptly explained, money hides behind a door called a problem. We hear people who like to declare, to anyone who will listen, that money does not buy happiness, yet they go on strike to demand a pay raise from their employer. They forget that poverty does not buy happiness either. Given the choice between wealth and poverty, how many would choose poverty? Because it is clearly better to have more money than not having enough. The purpose of money is not happiness but to pay bills, solve problems, help others, give gifts....

While money can do a lot of good around you, it can also do a lot of damage, destroy lives, divide families, and destroy an entire community. Money is a very formidable weapon. If we had to compare it to a modern weapon, we could easily compare it to an atomic weapon. For a long time, Christians have been misinformed about money, which has led to a certain phobia about wealth. Some go so far as to think that if they are rich, they will not be able to go to heaven since it is written that "it is easier for a camel to go through the eye of a needle than for a rich man to enter the kingdom of God." Access to the Kingdom of God is not given by money or wealth. But, as Jesus said to Nicodemus in John chapter 3, access to the kingdom of God is acquired by the new birth in Christ (the birth from above).

The usefulness of money is a fact, as is the danger it represents: it is the root of all evil. If money is an excellent servant, it is nonetheless a very bad master. God is not against the fact that we have a lot of money. On the contrary, He gives us the teachings on how to gain a lot of it and become rich. However, God's Word warns us against being led by money and recommends wisdom to counterbalance the power of money and learn how to use it well. Solomon's advice is very clear: "Wisdom is the principal thing; therefore get wisdom. And in all your getting, get understanding." Throughout the Scriptures we find:

- everything that can help us understand money, prosperity, and wealth
- how to get them
- how to handle or use them
- the dangers that can arise from a bad attitude or misuse of wealth
- the attitude we must develop toward them
- the role that wisdom plays in the whole process

This book does not contain everything that the Bible tells us about money, prosperity, and wealth. We are working on a second book that will present the summary of other biblical texts on certain other aspects of the same subject. The aim of this book is to make an inventory of the biblical texts that deal with money, prosperity, and wealth and to make a synopsis of them. We hope that this book will help readers in their meditation session, in accordance with Joshua 1:8: "This book of the law shall not depart out of thy mouth; but thou shalt meditate therein day and night, that thou mayest observe to do according to all that is written therein: for then thou shalt make thy way prosperous, and then thou shalt have good success" and Psalms 1:2-3, "But his delight is in the law of the LORD; and in his law doth he meditate day and night. And he shall be like a tree planted by the rivers of water, that brings forth his fruit in his season; his leaf also shall not wither; and whatever he does shall prosper."

Because as the psalmist David says: "The entrance of Your words gives light; It gives understanding to the simple" (Psalms 119:130).

May the Lord illuminate your understanding to become successful in all your ways.

Your comments and suggestions are important to us. Please send them to: j.pitterson23@gmail.com.

Part 1 – Money in the Bible

Chapter 1
Money in the Book of Genesis

Genesis 17:12-27

12 And he that is eight days old shall be circumcised among you, every man child in your generations, he that is born in the house, or bought with money of any stranger, which is not of thy seed.

13 He that is born in thy house, and he that is bought with thy money, must needs be circumcised: and my covenant shall be in your flesh for an everlasting covenant.

14 And the uncircumcised man child whose flesh of his foreskin is not circumcised, that soul shall be cut off from his people; he hath broken my covenant.

15 And God said unto Abraham, As for Sarai thy wife, thou shalt not call her name Sarai, but Sarah shall her name be.

16 And I will bless her, and give thee a son also of her: yea, I will bless her, and she shall be a mother of nations; kings of people shall be of her.

17 Then Abraham fell upon his face, and laughed, and said in his heart, Shall a child be born unto him that is an hundred years old? and shall Sarah, that is ninety years old, bear?

18 And Abraham said unto God, O that Ishmael might live before thee!

19 And God said, Sarah thy wife shall bear thee a son indeed; and thou shalt call his name Isaac: and I will establish my covenant with him for an everlasting covenant, and with his seed after him.

20 And as for Ishmael, I have heard thee: Behold, I have blessed him, and will make him fruitful, and will multiply him exceedingly; twelve princes shall he beget, and I will make him a great nation.

21 But my covenant will I establish with Isaac, which Sarah shall bear unto thee at this set time in the next year.

22 And he left off talking with him, and God went up from Abraham.

23 And Abraham took Ishmael his son, and all that were born in his house, and all that were bought with his money, every male among the men of Abraham's house; and circumcised the flesh of their foreskin in the selfsame day, as God had said unto him.

24 And Abraham was ninety years old and nine, when he was circumcised in the flesh of his foreskin.

25 And Ishmael his son was thirteen years old, when he was circumcised in the flesh of his foreskin.

26 In the selfsame day was Abraham circumcised, and Ishmael his son.

27 And all the men of his house, born in the house, and bought with money of the stranger, were circumcised with him.

Summary

In establishing his covenant with Abraham, God ordered him to circumcise, as a sign of the covenant, all the men in his house from the age of 8 days. This includes Abraham himself and all those born in his house or acquired with money. Everyone who is old enough to be circumcised, but is not, should be put to death. God takes the opportunity to change Sarai's name to Sarah and promises Abraham that, despite their advanced age, Sarah will bear him a son and that nations will come from her womb.

It is important to note that this is the first time the word 'money' is used in the Bible—God used it to refer to the method of payment for a transaction that seemed common to the era.

Genesis 23:9-16

9 That he may give me the cave of Machpelah, which he hath, which is in the end of his field; for as much money as it is worth he shall give it me for a possession of a buryingplace amongst you.

10 And Ephron dwelt among the children of Heth: and Ephron the Hittite answered Abraham in the audience of the children of Heth, even of all that went in at the gate of his city, saying,

11 Nay, my lord, hear me: the field give I thee, and the cave that is therein, I give it thee; in the presence of the sons of my people give I it thee: bury thy dead.

12 And Abraham bowed down himself before the people of the land.

13 And he spake unto Ephron in the audience of the people of the land, saying, But if thou wilt give it, I pray thee, hear me: I will give thee money for the field; take it of me, and I will bury my dead there.

14 And Ephron answered Abraham, saying unto him,

15 My lord, hearken unto me: the land is worth four hundred shekels of silver; what is that betwixt me and thee? bury therefore thy dead.

16 And Abraham hearkened unto Ephron; and Abraham weighed to Ephron the silver, which he had named in the audience of the sons of Heth, four hundred shekels of silver, current money with the merchant.

Summary

Following the death of Sarah, Abraham went to the sons of Heth with the aim of purchasing the cave of Machpelah in order to erect a burial place for his late wife and, eventually, their descendants. Ephron, who owned the cave and an adjacent field, offered to give them to Abraham for free. He politely refused and asked him to estimate the price. Ephron ultimately valued the property at 400 shekels of silver. Abraham, without discussing it with him, paid him the entire amount on the spot in the presence of everyone.

This text takes advantage of Sarah's death to present to us the first real estate transaction reported in the Bible.

Genesis 31:14-16

14 And Rachel and Leah answered and said unto him, Is there yet any portion or inheritance for us in our father's house?

15 Are we not counted of him strangers? for he hath sold us, and hath quite devoured also our money.

16 For all the riches which God hath taken from our father, that is ours, and our children's: now then, whatsoever God hath said unto thee, do.

Summary

Following Laban's change of attitude, God asks Jacob, in a dream, to leave Laban's house and return to his native country. Jacob reunites his wives, Leah and Rachel, reminds them of how their father deceived him on many occasions, going so far as to change his salary ten times despite his loyalty, and tells them that God asked him to return to his country. For their part, Leah and Rachel tell him of their frustration, their feeling of marginalization, and how their father, Laban, mistreated them by selling them and using up their money. They recognize that the departure is justified and ask him to do everything God has ordered him, expressing all their support. In this text, money seems to be used as a synonym for inheritance.

Genesis 33:17-19

17 And Jacob journeyed to Succoth, and built him an house, and made booths for his cattle: therefore the name of the place is called Succoth.

18 And Jacob came to Shalem, a city of Shechem, which is in the land of Canaan, when he came from Padanaram; and pitched his tent before the city.

19 And he bought a parcel of a field, where he had spread his tent, at the hand of the children of Hamor, Shechem's father, for an hundred pieces of money.

Summary

After his reconciliation with his brother Esau, Jacob goes to Succoth, where he builds a house for his family and facilities for his livestock. Then he goes to the city of Shechem, in the land of Canaan. There, he bought a field from the descendants of Hamor, father of Shechem, for a hundred pieces of money and built himself tents and an altar to the Lord.

Genesis 42:25-28, 35

25 Then Joseph commanded to fill their sacks with corn, and to restore every man's money into his sack, and to give them provision for the way: and thus did he unto them.

26 And they laded their asses with the corn, and departed thence.

27 And as one of them opened his sack to give his ass provender in the inn, he espied his money; for, behold, it was in his sack's mouth.

28 And he said unto his brethren, My money is restored; and, lo, it is even in my sack: and their heart failed them, and they were afraid, saying one to another, What is this that God hath done unto us?

35 And it came to pass as they emptied their sacks, that, behold, every man's bundle of money was in his sack: and when both they and their father saw the bundles of money, they were afraid.

Summary

A great famine hits the entire land of Canaan, and Jacob decides to send all his sons to Egypt to buy wheat, with the exception of his youngest son, Benjamin. In Egypt, they were immediately recognized by Joseph, who had since become Pharaoh's second-in-command. He had them imprisoned, accusing them of being spies. For their part, they do not recognize Joseph, whom they believe to have been dead for a long time. To defend themselves, they admit that they are twelve brothers, all sons of the same father, one of whom is dead (in this case, Joseph, whom they believe to be dead), and the youngest remained with their father. To clear them of all suspicion, Joseph offers to sell them wheat on the condition that he keeps Simeon in prison and that they bring back their youngest brother to him.

Following their agreement, Joseph ordered his servants to fill their bags with wheat and then put everyone's money back in their bags and let them go. When they return, they explain to their father everything that happened to them and notice that everyone's money is in their bag.

In this passage, money is used in commerce as a means of payment for a business transaction.

Genesis 43:12-23

12 And take double money in your hand; and the money that was brought again in the mouth of your sacks, carry it again in your hand; peradventure it was an oversight:

13 Take also your brother, and arise, go again unto the man:

14 And God Almighty give you mercy before the man, that he may send away your other brother, and Benjamin. If I be bereaved of my children, I am bereaved.

15 And the men took that present, and they took double money in their hand and Benjamin; and rose up, and went down to Egypt, and stood before Joseph.

16 And when Joseph saw Benjamin with them, he said to the ruler of his house, Bring these men home, and slay, and make ready; for these men shall dine with me at noon.

17 And the man did as Joseph bade; and the man brought the men into Joseph's house.

18 And the men were afraid, because they were brought into Joseph's house; and they said, Because of the money that was returned in our

sacks at the first time are we brought in; that he may seek occasion against us, and fall upon us, and take us for bondmen, and our asses.

19 And they came near to the steward of Joseph's house, and they communed with him at the door of the house,

20 And said, O sir, we came indeed down at the first time to buy food:

21 And it came to pass, when we came to the inn, that we opened our sacks, and, behold, every man's money was in the mouth of his sack, our money in full weight: and we have brought it again in our hand.

22 And other money have we brought down in our hands to buy food: we cannot tell who put our money in our sacks.

23 And he said, Peace be to you, fear not: your God, and the God of your father, hath given you treasure in your sacks: I had your money. And he brought Simeon out unto them.

Summary

Having run out of grain, Jacob finally agrees to let Benjamin go to Egypt with his brothers. He asks them to bring double the amount of money to return the money they had found in their bags. He also asks them to take balsam, honey, spices, myrrh, pistachios, and almonds from the best productions of the country as a present to the Egyptian sovereign (Joseph). When they returned to Egypt, Joseph ordered his steward to welcome them into his home as guests and prepare a feast, as they would eat with him. Seeing that they were invited to Joseph's house, they were frightened and told each other that they were going to be killed. In this context, they confide to the steward that they brought twice the necessary amount in order to return the money they had found in their bags. The steward replies that, for his part, the money has been collected and that he thinks their God placed the money in their bags. Joseph's brothers were never able to identify him.

Genesis 44:1-8

1 And he commanded the steward of his house, saying, Fill the men's sacks with food, as much as they can carry, and put every man's money in his sack's mouth.

2 And put my cup, the silver cup, in the sack's mouth of the youngest, and his corn money. And he did according to the word that Joseph had spoken.

3 As soon as the morning was light, the men were sent away, they and their asses.

4 And when they were gone out of the city, and not yet far off, Joseph said unto his steward, Up, follow after the men; and when thou dost overtake them, say unto them, Wherefore have ye rewarded evil for good?

5 Is not this it in which my lord drinketh, and whereby indeed he divineth? ye have done evil in so doing.

6 And he overtook them, and he spake unto them these same words.

7 And they said unto him, Wherefore saith my lord these words? God forbid that thy servants should do according to this thing:

8 Behold, the money, which we found in our sacks' mouths, we brought again unto thee out of the land of Canaan: how then should we steal out of thy lord's house silver or gold?

Summary

Joseph orders his steward to fill the bags of each of his brothers with wheat, to place their money in their respective bags, and to put his cup in Benjamin's bag. The next day, very early, they left Joseph's house and traveled toward Canaan. After they left the city, Joseph asked his steward to pursue them and accuse them of stealing his cup. The steward goes after them, catches them after they leave the city, and accuses them of theft. They completely deny this accusation and agree that whoever is found with the cup will become the slave of the Egyptian Ruler (Joseph). The steward searches their bags, starting with the eldest, and finds the cup in Benjamin's bag. Faced with this observation, they are all confused and distraught. This text shows Joseph's desire to assess his brothers' remorse for their past actions and their loyalty to Benjamin, as well as their willingness to protect and defend each other in the face of adversity. It should be noted that the money placed in their bags was not mentioned during the search.

Genesis 47:14-19

14 And Joseph gathered up all the money that was found in the land of Egypt, and in the land of Canaan, for the corn which they bought: and Joseph brought the money into Pharaoh's house.

15 And when money failed in the land of Egypt, and in the land of Canaan, all the Egyptians came unto Joseph, and said, Give us bread: for why should we die in thy presence? for the money faileth.

16 And Joseph said, Give your cattle; and I will give you for your cattle, if money fail.

17 And they brought their cattle unto Joseph: and Joseph gave them bread in exchange for horses, and for the flocks, and for the cattle of the herds, and for the asses: and he fed them with bread for all their cattle for that year.

18 When that year was ended, they came unto him the second year, and said unto him, We will not hide it from my lord, how that our money is spent; my lord also hath our herds of cattle; there is not ought left in the sight of my lord, but our bodies, and our lands:

19 Wherefore shall we die before thine eyes, both we and our land? buy us and our land for bread, and we and our land will be servants unto Pharaoh: and give us seed, that we may live, and not die, that the land be not desolate.

J. Pitterson

Summary

The famine increases throughout the land of Egypt and the land of Canaan. Joseph, who was appointed Pharon's second in command to manage the crisis, built up large reserves throughout the country. People come from all over to Joseph to buy grain. When they run out of money, Joseph offers to trade their livestock for grain and they willingly agree. When they had no more animals left, they sold their land and then themselves to Joseph to serve Pharaoh in exchange for grain. Thus, Joseph appropriated all the lands except those of the priests, who had an exemption, and pocketed all the money from Egypt for the benefit of Pharaoh. This allowed Joseph to relocate the people to the cities and provide them with seeds to plant to ensure their sustenance during the famine, while requiring them to pay a fifth of the harvest to Pharaoh. This passage highlights Joseph's leadership, management ability, and business acumen.

Chapter 2
Money in the Book of Exodus

Exodus 12:43-45

43 And the Lord said unto Moses and Aaron, This is the ordinance of the passover: There shall no stranger eat thereof:

44 But every man's servant that is bought for money, when thou hast circumcised him, then shall he eat thereof.

45 A foreigner and an hired servant shall not eat thereof.

Summary

By communicating the Passover ordinance to Moses and Aaron, God indicates who may participate in the Passover meal. It stipulates that no uncircumcised foreigner can participate, including the slave acquired for money, the inhabitant, and the mercenary. However, if any of them wish to celebrate Passover, they must first ensure that every male in their household submits to circumcision, just like a native-born Israelite.

This text highlights the importance of circumcision as a sign of the covenant between God and Israel and emphasizes the exclusivity of Passover observance for those who are part of the covenant community. It also shows that the slave trade, which had been mentioned in the Bible since Joseph was sold by his brothers, still continued at the time.

Exodus 21:7-11

7 And if a man sell his daughter to be a maidservant, she shall not go out as the menservants do.

8 If she please not her master, who hath betrothed her to himself, then shall he let her be redeemed: to sell her unto a strange nation he shall have no power, seeing he hath dealt deceitfully with her.

9 And if he have betrothed her unto his son, he shall deal with her after the manner of daughters.

10 If he take him another wife; her food, her raiment, and her duty of marriage, shall he not diminish.

11 And if he do not these three unto her, then shall she go out free without money.

Summary

This text presents the laws regarding how slaves, both men and women, should be treated in ancient Israel. Exodus 21: 1-6 presents the law on male slaves, while verses 7-11 discuss the treatment of female slaves. It stipulates that if a father sells his daughter into slavery, she will not be freed after six years of service like male slaves are. She may be intended to be the wife of her buyer or that of his son.

- If the master or buyer is not happy with her, he must allow her to be bought by someone else. However, he cannot sell her to foreigners.

- If the master takes her as a wife for his son, he must treat her as his daughter.

- If the master takes another wife, he must still provide for her needs in terms of food, clothing, and marital rights.

If the master fails in any of these responsibilities, the woman can go free without paying him any money. This suggests the idea that at any time, the woman can buy back her freedom, with the agreement of her master, if she has enough to pay the master his money.

This passage shows that slave women had certain legal protections, ensuring that they were not treated unfairly and that they had certain rights within the household.

Exodus 21:20-21

20 And if a man smite his servant, or his maid, with a rod, and he die under his hand; he shall be surely punished.

21 Notwithstanding, if he continue a day or two, he shall not be punished: for he is his money.

Summary

This text presents us with the legal prescription concerning the consequences for a person who strikes his slave, male or female, with a rod, resulting in his death. If the slave dies instantly, the master must be punished. However, if the slave survives a day or two before dying, the master will not be punished since it involves his money. The word money here is synonymous with property. This introduces the idea of a transfer of ownership. What someone acquires with his money changes the owner and automatically becomes his property.

This passage reflects the cultural norms of the time, where slaves were considered property, and sets limits on the severity of punishments for those who harm their slaves. It is important to emphasize that this text does not reflect the overall teaching of the Bible on the subject. A synopsis of the Bible's teaching regarding slavery can be found in the footnote [1] [2].

---

[1] https://www.gotquestions.org/Bible-slavery.html

[2] https://www.la-croix.com/Abonnes/Theologie/Quel-sens-lesclavage-Bible-2018-06-11-1700946147 (may be translated from French to English)

Exodus 21:28-32

28 If an ox gore a man or a woman, that they die: then the ox shall be surely stoned, and his flesh shall not be eaten; but the owner of the ox shall be quit.

29 But if the ox were wont to push with his horn in time past, and it hath been testified to his owner, and he hath not kept him in, but that he hath killed a man or a woman; the ox shall be stoned, and his owner also shall be put to death.

30 If there be laid on him a sum of money, then he shall give for the ransom of his life whatsoever is laid upon him.

31 Whether he have gored a son, or have gored a daughter, according to this judgment shall it be done unto him.

32 If the ox shall push a manservant or a maidservant; he shall give unto their master thirty shekels of silver, and the ox shall be stoned.

Summary

This passage describes the legal provisions for a person killed or injured by an ox and the compensation owed to victims. If an ox gores someone and death follows, it must be stoned and its meat cannot be eaten. The owner of the ox will not be held responsible and will therefore not be punished. On the other hand, if the owner knew that the ox was showing signs of violence and could kill someone and did not take the necessary steps to restrain it properly, he would be put to death and the ox would be stoned. If the owner is forced to pay in exchange for his life, whatever the amount, he will have to pay it.

If the ox injures a slave, it will be stoned and its owner must pay thirty shekels of silver to the slave's master. The shekel of silver refers to a type of currency used in trade at the time.

Exodus 21:33-34

33 And if a man shall open a pit, or if a man shall dig a pit, and not cover it, and an ox or an ass fall therein;

34 The owner of the pit shall make it good, and give money unto the owner of them; and the dead beast shall be his.

Summary

This is about how to deal with the situation where someone leaves a pit uncovered or digs one and doesn't cover it, and an ox falls into it. If the ox dies, the owner of the pit is held responsible. In this case, he must take the corpse for himself and pay the owner of the ox its value in money. This highlights the importance of taking precautions to keep others safe, even on one's own property, and holds individuals responsible for any negligence that results in harm to others or their property.

Exodus 21:35-36

35 And if one man's ox hurt another's, that he die; then they shall sell the live ox, and divide the money of it; and the dead ox also they shall divide.

36 Or if it be known that the ox hath used to push in time past, and his owner hath not kept him in; he shall surely pay ox for ox; and the dead shall be his own.

Summary

This text presents us with the legal way to deal with the scenario in which one person's ox kills another person's. If someone's ox gores the ox of another person, resulting in its death, both owners must sell the live ox and divide the money between them. Then they will share the dead ox.

However, if the live ox had a known history of violence and its owner failed to take appropriate precautions, then the owner of the live ox must fully compensate the owner of the dead ox and the dead ox becomes his or hers.

Exodus 22:7-8

7 If a man shall deliver unto his neighbour money or stuff to keep, and it be stolen out of the man's house; if the thief be found, let him pay double.

8 If the thief be not found, then the master of the house shall be brought unto the judges, to see whether he have put his hand unto his neighbour's goods.

Summary

This text illustrates the scenario where a person entrusts money or goods to their neighbor and the latter keeps them at home. If the house is broken into and the thief is caught, he must pay double what he stole. If the thief is not caught, the owner must, in this case, take an oath before God that he did not take advantage of the situation and he would not be held responsible for the theft.

This law highlights the importance of honesty and responsibility in human relationships and aims to guarantee fair treatment for both the owner of the property and the person in charge of it.

Exodus 22:16-17

16 And if a man entice a maid that is not betrothed, and lie with her, he shall surely endow her to be his wife.

17 If her father utterly refuse to give her unto him, he shall pay money according to the dowry of virgins.

Summary

In this text, the law states that if a man seduces and sleeps with a virgin girl who is not engaged, that man must pay her father a dowry and then marry her. If the father refuses to give him his daughter in marriage, the man will then have to pay in money the value of the dowry for virgins.

Exodus 22:25 If thou lend money to any of my people that is poor by thee, thou shalt not be to him as an usurer, neither shalt thou lay upon him usury.

Summary

The text emphasizes that anyone who lends money to someone in need should not behave like a creditor and demand interest from them. This law reflects a concern for the well-being of the most deprived and encourages generosity and assistance without exploiting the vulnerability of the weakest.

Exodus 30:13-16

13 This they shall give, every one that passeth among them that are numbered, half a shekel after the shekel of the sanctuary: (a shekel is twenty gerahs:) an half shekel shall be the offering of the Lord.

14 Every one that passeth among them that are numbered, from twenty years old and above, shall give an offering unto the Lord.

15 The rich shall not give more, and the poor shall not give less than half a shekel, when they give an offering unto the Lord, to make an atonement for your souls.

16 And thou shalt take the atonement money of the children of Israel, and shalt appoint it for the service of the tabernacle of the congregation; that it may be a memorial unto the children of Israel before the Lord, to make an atonement for your souls.

Summary

During the numbering of the people in the desert, God asked Moses to collect an offering of half a shekel, according to the shekel of the sanctuary, for the work of building and fitting out the tabernacle of the congregation. This offering is taken from all men participating in the numbering from the age of 20 and above. The amount of the offering is the same for both the rich and the poor, symbolizing that, in this context, all are equal before God. It is called a redemption offering and is given in remembrance of the redemption of their souls. This passage highlights the importance of financial support in serving God among the Israelites.

Chapter 3
Money in the Book of Leviticus

Leviticus 22:10-11

10 There shall no stranger eat of the holy thing: a sojourner of the priest, or an hired servant, shall not eat of the holy thing.

11 But if the priest buy any soul with his money, he shall eat of it, and he that is born in his house: they shall eat of his meat.

Summary

In presenting to the people of Israel the law on holy things, God mentions that everything offered in sacrifice to Him is decreed holy. He declares that, apart from the priest, foreigners, hirelings, and those who dwell with the priest cannot eat holy things. However, he who was born in the house of the priest and the slave he bought with money may eat of it. This shows the sacred nature of the offerings and the importance of maintaining the distinction between the sacred and the common.

Leviticus 25:35-37

35 And if thy brother be waxen poor, and fallen in decay with thee; then thou shalt relieve him: yea, though he be a stranger, or a sojourner; that he may live with thee.

36 Take thou no usury of him, or increase: but fear thy God; that thy brother may live with thee.

37 Thou shalt not give him thy money upon usury, nor lend him thy victuals for increase.

Summary

God prescribes here the management of human relations to the people of Israel and, above all, particularly to support those who are less fortunate and weak, foreigners, and those who live in the country. God commands the people of Israel to help these people financially without exploiting their situation. If you lend them money, do not charge them interest or lend them provisions with usury. This passage illustrates the importance of compassion, generosity, and fair treatment within the community, especially toward those who are less fortunate.

Leviticus 25:47-54

47 And if a sojourner or stranger wax rich by thee, and thy brother that dwelleth by him wax poor, and sell himself unto the stranger or sojourner by thee, or to the stock of the stranger's family:

48 After that he is sold he may be redeemed again; one of his brethren may redeem him:

49 Either his uncle, or his uncle's son, may redeem him, or any that is nigh of kin unto him of his family may redeem him; or if he be able, he may redeem himself.

50 And he shall reckon with him that bought him from the year that he was sold to him unto the year of jubile: and the price of his sale shall be according unto the number of years, according to the time of an hired servant shall it be with him.

51 If there be yet many years behind, according unto them he shall give again the price of his redemption out of the money that he was bought for.

52 And if there remain but few years unto the year of jubile, then he shall count with him, and according unto his years shall he give him again the price of his redemption.

53 And as a yearly hired servant shall he be with him: and the other shall not rule with rigour over him in thy sight.

54 And if he be not redeemed in these years, then he shall go out in the year of jubile, both he, and his children with him.

Summary

In this passage, God makes legal provision for situations when an Israelite becomes impoverished and sells himself into slavery to a stranger or a member of a stranger's family. In this scenario, the Israelite retains the right to be redeemed, either by a close relative acting as his redeemer or by himself if he were to have the necessary resources. The cost of the buyout is determined based on the lower cost, calculated between the number of years remaining until the year of jubilee and the number of years spent in service. If the Israelite cannot be redeemed, he and his children must be freed during the year of jubilee, for the Israelites are not to be treated as slaves but as hirelings and travelers before the Lord.

This law emphasizes God's concern for the well-being and dignity of his people, ensuring that even in times of financial hardship, they are not permanently deprived of their freedom or rights.

Leviticus 27:14-15

14 And when a man shall sanctify his house to be holy unto the Lord, then the priest shall estimate it, whether it be good or bad: as the priest shall estimate it, so shall it stand.

15 And if he that sanctified it will redeem his house, then he shall add the fifth part of the money of thy estimation unto it, and it shall be his.

Summary

This passage deals with the question of the redemption of houses consecrated to the Lord. If someone dedicates his house to the Lord, the priest is responsible for evaluating it, and they will stick to the cost estimated by the priest. If the owner of the house wants to buy it back later, he will have to pay the money estimated by the priest plus an additional fifth.

Leviticus 27:16-19

16 And if a man shall sanctify unto the Lord some part of a field of his possession, then thy estimation shall be according to the seed thereof: an homer of barley seed shall be valued at fifty shekels of silver.

17 If he sanctify his field from the year of jubile, according to thy estimation it shall stand.

18 But if he sanctify his field after the jubile, then the priest shall reckon unto him the money according to the years that remain, even unto the year of the jubile, and it shall be abated from thy estimation.

19 And if he that sanctified the field will in any wise redeem it, then he shall add the fifth part of the money of thy estimation unto it, and it shall be assured to him.

Summary

This passage concerns the dedication of agricultural fields to the Lord. If someone dedicates part of his field to the Lord, its value is determined according to the quantity of seed needed to sow it, knowing that a homer of barley seed is valued at fifty shekels of silver. If the field is dedicated during the jubilee year, the initial estimate will be adhered to. If it is made after the jubilee, the priest will make an estimate based on the number of years remaining until the jubilee and a deduction will be made from the initial estimate. If the owner of the field wishes to buy it back later, he must pay its estimated money plus an additional fifth.

Chapter 4
Money in the Book of Numbers

Numbers 3:42-51

42 And Moses numbered, as the Lord commanded him, all the firstborn among the children of Israel.

43 And all the firstborn males by the number of names, from a month old and upward, of those that were numbered of them, were twenty and two thousand two hundred and threescore and thirteen.

44 And the Lord spake unto Moses, saying,

45 Take the Levites instead of all the firstborn among the children of Israel, and the cattle of the Levites instead of their cattle; and the Levites shall be mine: I am the Lord.

46 And for those that are to be redeemed of the two hundred and threescore and thirteen of the firstborn of the children of Israel, which are more than the Levites;

47 Thou shalt even take five shekels apiece by the poll, after the shekel of the sanctuary shalt thou take them: (the shekel is twenty gerahs:)

48 And thou shalt give the money, wherewith the odd number of them is to be redeemed, unto Aaron and to his sons.

49 And Moses took the redemption money of them that were over and above them that were redeemed by the Levites:

50 Of the firstborn of the children of Israel took he the money; a thousand three hundred and threescore and five shekels, after the shekel of the sanctuary:

51 And Moses gave the money of them that were redeemed unto Aaron and to his sons, according to the word of the Lord, as the Lord commanded Moses.

Summary

God asks Moses to successively enumerate the Levites and the firstborn sons of Israel aged one month and over. This reveals that the total number of Levites amounts to 22,000, while the number of firstborn sons is 22,273. Then Moses is asked to place all the Levites at the permanent disposal of God in place of the firstborn son of Israel. Since the number of the firstborn sons exceeds the number of the Levites by 273, God commands the redemption of these 273 firstborn sons at the rate of five shekels of silver per head and to give the money to Aaron and his sons for the service of the tabernacle. This passage highlights the setting apart of the Levites for service in the sanctuary of God.

Numbers 18:11-16

11 And this is thine; the heave offering of their gift, with all the wave offerings of the children of Israel: I have given them unto thee, and to thy sons and to thy daughters with thee, by a statute for ever: every one that is clean in thy house shall eat of it.

12 All the best of the oil, and all the best of the wine, and of the wheat, the firstfruits of them which they shall offer unto the Lord, them have I given thee.

13 And whatsoever is first ripe in the land, which they shall bring unto the Lord, shall be thine; every one that is clean in thine house shall eat of it.

14 Every thing devoted in Israel shall be thine.

15 Every thing that openeth the matrix in all flesh, which they bring unto the Lord, whether it be of men or beasts, shall be thine: nevertheless the firstborn of man shalt thou surely redeem, and the firstling of unclean beasts shalt thou redeem.

16 And those that are to be redeemed from a month old shalt thou redeem, according to thine estimation, for the money of five shekels, after the shekel of the sanctuary, which is twenty gerahs.

Summary

In this text, God instructs Aaron on the use of the offerings collected from the people and entrusts him and his sons, by a perpetual law, with the charge of all the offerings dedicated to the Lord. Among his offerings, Aaron is entitled to:

- most holy offerings which are not reserved for the fire, which only he and his sons can consume .
- gifts presented by elevation and by waving them from side to side, which he, his sons, and his daughters are entitled to by perpetual law. Whoever is pure in his house may eat it.
- first fruits of all agricultural products. Whoever is pure in his house may eat it.
- everything that is forbidden in Israel, of which anyone who is pure in his house may eat.
- firstborn of all flesh, both men and animals, are his. However, he must, from the age of one month, redeem for money the first born of man, as well as that of an impure animal at the price of five shekels of silver.

Chapter 5
Money in the Book of Deuteronomy

Deuteronomy 2:4-7

4 And command the people, saying, "You are about to pass through the territory of your brethren, the descendants of Esau, who live in Seir; and they will be afraid of you. Therefore watch yourselves carefully.

5 Do not meddle with them, for I will not give you any of their land, no, not so much as one footstep, because I have given Mount Seir to Esau as a possession.

6 You shall buy food from them with money, that you may eat; and you shall also buy water from them with money, that you may drink.

7 "For the Lord your God has blessed you in all the work of your hand. He knows your trudging through this great wilderness. These forty years the Lord your God has been with you; you have lacked nothing." '

Summary

The text here tells us that after Israel left the mountains of Seir, they marched near the border of the sons of Esau, brother of Jacob. God orders the people not to attack them or provoke incidents with them and to buy at a price of money all the provisions they consume, including water. He assured them that he would not give them even a foot from the land he had given to Esau because it was his inheritance. God reminds them of how He provided for them for forty years in the desert, ensuring that they lacked nothing during their journey. This passage highlights God's sovereignty over the land and His provision for His people as they journeyed toward their own inheritance.

Deuteronomy 2:26-30

26 "And I sent messengers from the Wilderness of Kedemoth to Sihon king of Heshbon, with words of peace, saying,

27 'Let me pass through your land; I will keep strictly to the road, and I will turn neither to the right nor to the left.

28 You shall sell me food for money, that I may eat, and give me water for money, that I may drink; only let me pass through on foot,

29 just as the descendants of Esau who dwell in Seir and the Moabites who dwell in Ar did for me, until I cross the Jordan to the land which the Lord our God is giving us.'

30 "But Sihon king of Heshbon would not let us pass through, for the Lord your God hardened his spirit and made his heart obstinate, that He might deliver him into your hand, as it is this day.

Summary

Moses sends messengers to Sihon, king of Heshbon, to ask permission to cross his country with the people. He promises to stay on the main road, without deviating there, and to buy for money the food and water that they will consume during their passage. But King Sihon refused to let them pass through his territory because God had made his spirit inflexible and hardened his heart in order to deliver him into the hands of Israel.

Deuteronomy 14:24-26

24 But if the journey is too long for you, so that you are not able to carry the tithe, or if the place where the Lord your God chooses to put His name is too far from you, when the Lord your God has blessed you,

25 then you shall exchange it for money, take the money in your hand, and go to the place which the Lord your God chooses.

26 And you shall spend that money for whatever your heart desires: for oxen or sheep, for wine or similar drink, for whatever your heart desires; you shall eat there before the Lord your God, and you shall rejoice, you and your household.

Summary

In this passage, Moses conveys to the people God's ordinances concerning tithing, especially to those far from the place of worship. These people are allowed to exchange their tithes, which are agricultural and livestock products, for money and then bring that money to the place of worship. There, they can use it to buy whatever pleases them, whether it is livestock, wine, or strong drinks, in order to celebrate and eat with their families and the Levites who live among them and who have no heritage of their own.

This passage highlights that financial blessings come from God and that it is important to worship the Lord and celebrate His blessings together with joy and generosity.

Deuteronomy 21:10-14

10 "When you go out to war against your enemies, and the Lord your God delivers them into your hand, and you take them captive,

11 and you see among the captives a beautiful woman, and desire her and would take her for your wife,

12 then you shall bring her home to your house, and she shall shave her head and trim her nails.

13 She shall put off the clothes of her captivity, remain in your house, and mourn her father and her mother a full month; after that you may go in to her and be her husband, and she shall be your wife.

14 And it shall be, if you have no delight in her, then you shall set her free, but you certainly shall not sell her for money; you shall not treat her brutally, because you have humbled her.

Summary

In this text, Moses transmits instructions to the people regarding the treatment of women captured in war. An Israelite soldier who identifies a beautiful woman among the captives and who wishes to marry her must first of all release her from among the captives and bring her to his home. There, she will shed her captivity clothing, shave her head, cut her nails, and mourn her parents for a full month. The man will not be able to sleep with her while she is grieving and adapting to her new reality. At the end of the mourning period, the man will be able to sleep with her and she will become his wife. If he no longer likes her, he must let her go free. He cannot treat her brutally, like a slave, or sell her for money because she has been humiliated.

This passage highlights compassion and respect for women, even in the context of war, and their dignity and rights must be respected.

Deuteronomy 23:19-20

19 "You shall not charge interest to your brother—interest on money or food or anything that is lent out at interest.

20 To a foreigner you may charge interest, but to your brother you shall not charge interest, that the Lord your God may bless you in all to which you set your hand in the land which you are entering to possess.

Summary

In this passage, Moses tells the Israelites that it is forbidden to charge interest on loans of money, food, or anything else that can be lent to their fellow Israelites. However, they are allowed to charge interest on loans given to foreigners. This regulation highlights the importance of fairness and compassion within the community, ensuring that lending practices do not exploit or burden fellow Israelites in need.

Chapter 6
Money in the Book of Judges

Judges 5: 19-20

19 The kings came and fought, then fought the kings of Canaan in Taanach by the waters of Megiddo; they took no gain of money.

20 They fought from heaven; the stars in their courses fought against Sisera.

Summary

In this text, Deborah, prophetess and judge of Israel, sings of the battle against Sisera, who was the commander of the army of Jabin, king of the land of Canaan. It describes how the kings of Canaan fought at Taanah, near the waters of Megiddo, but could not win any money as spoils of war, which, in other words, reflects their defeat. Deborah contrasts this with the bravery of the Israelite warriors, who fought with determination and defeated the army of Sisera and the nine hundred iron chariots that were their pride. They were able to kill all the soldiers and then force Sisera to abandon his personal chariot, flee on foot, and go into hiding. He will be killed in his sleep by a woman. Thus, it brings shame to the entire land of Canaan.

Judges 16: 18-19

18 When Delilah saw that he had told her all his heart, she sent and called for the lords of the Philistines, saying, "Come up once more, for he has told me all his heart." So the lords of the Philistines came up to her and brought the money in their hand.

19 Then she lulled him to sleep on her knees, and called for a man and had him shave off the seven locks of his head. Then [c]she began to torment him, and his strength left him.

Summary

After having failed three times to extract from Samson the secret of his strength, Delilah strives to question him and continually bothers him every day on the subject, to the point of exasperating him. Samson ends up confessing to her that he was consecrated to God in his mother's womb and, therefore, he must not shave his head. In fact, he has never shaved his head since birth because his extraordinary strength comes from his hair. Convinced that Samson had confessed his secret to her, she summoned the princes of the Philistines to come and seize him. While waiting for the princes to arrive, she puts him to sleep on her knees, shaves his head, and does things to him that, in his sleep, deeply distress and weaken him. When the Philistine princes arrive and bring her money, Delilah wakes Samson by telling him that the Philistines are there. But, having lost his strength, he cannot defend himself, as in previous times. He is thus captured and becomes a prisoner of the Philistines.

Judges 17:1-4

1 And there was a man of mount Ephraim, whose name was Micah.

2 And he said unto his mother, The eleven hundred shekels of silver that were taken from thee, about which thou cursedst, and spakest of also in mine ears, behold, the silver is with me; I took it. And his mother said, Blessed be thou of the Lord, my son.

3 And when he had restored the eleven hundred shekels of silver to his mother, his mother said, I had wholly dedicated the silver unto the Lord from my hand for my son, to make a graven image and a molten image: now therefore I will restore it unto thee.

4 Yet he restored the money unto his mother; and his mother took two hundred shekels of silver, and gave them to the founder, who made thereof a graven image and a molten image: and they were in the house of Micah.

MONEY IN THE BIBLE

Summary

The mother of Micah, a man from the mountainous region of Ephraim, is robbed of 1100 shekels of silver without being able to identify who took it. In reaction, in the presence of her son, she makes imprecations and curses the one who took her money. But it happens that later, Micah returns to his mother and gives her back the entire missing sum, confessing to her that he had taken the money. Visibly happy and satisfied, she blesses her son, dedicates all the money to God, and uses it to make two portraits of Micah: a graven image and a molded image.

This passage highlights the confusion that raged at this time when the people were completely left to their own devices. Without a political leader and without a spiritual guide, everyone did what they pleased, paying no attention to the laws and ordinances of God.

Chapter 7
Money in the Books of Kings

1 Kings 21: 2-6

2 So Ahab spoke to Naboth, saying, "Give me your vineyard, that I may have it for a vegetable garden, because it is near, next to my house; and for it I will give you a vineyard better than it. Or, if it seems good to you, I will give you its worth in money."

3 But Naboth said to Ahab, "The Lord forbid that I should give the inheritance of my fathers to you!"

4 So Ahab went into his house sullen and displeased because of the word which Naboth the Jezreelite had spoken to him; for he had said, "I will not give you the inheritance of my fathers." And he lay down on his bed, and turned away his face, and would eat no food.

5 But Jezebel his wife came to him, and said to him, "Why is your spirit so sullen that you eat no food?"

6 He said to her, "Because I spoke to Naboth the Jezreelite, and said to him, 'Give me your vineyard for money; or else, if it pleases you, I will give you another vineyard for it.' And he answered, 'I will not give you my vineyard.' "

Summary

Ahab, king of Samaria, covets Naboth's vineyard, which is located right next to the royal palace, in order to make a vegetable garden. To acquire it, he offers to exchange it for a much better vineyard or for its value in money. Naboth kindly refuses to give it to him because it is a family heirloom that he feels obliged to preserve. If he separated from it, it would be an offense to his ancestors. Sad and angry at Naboth's refusal to sell him the vineyard, Ahab returns home, takes refuge in his bed, and eats nothing.

1 Kings 21: 15-16

15 And it came to pass, when Jezebel heard that Naboth had been stoned and was dead, that Jezebel said to Ahab, "Arise, take possession of the vineyard of Naboth the Jezreelite, which he refused to give you for money; for Naboth is not alive, but dead."

16 So it was, when Ahab heard that Naboth was dead, that Ahab got up and went down to take possession of the vineyard of Naboth the Jezreelite.

Summary

Queen Jezebel, Ahab's wife, learns of the king's displeasure with Naboth's refusal to sell him his vineyard. She comforts him and promises to fulfill his desire by giving him possession of this vineyard. Thereupon, she sets up an assassination plan against Naboth, the execution of which she personally supervises until its success. Falsely accused of cursing God and the king according to Jezebel's instructions, Naboth is judged by the elders and the nobles, condemned to death, and then stoned. Having learned of Naboth's death, Jezebel runs to tell Ahab the news and invites him to go and take possession of this vineyard that Naboth did not want to sell to him. Hearing of Naboth's death, Ahab quickly got up and went to the vineyard to take possession of it.

This passage illustrates the manipulation, corruption, and deception that characterize Jezebel's actions to satisfy Ahab's desires.

It also highlights the king's tacit approval of the queen's actions by allowing himself to be blinded by his desires to the point of becoming a murderer and a thief in the eyes of God.

2 Kings 5:25-27

25 Now he went in and stood before his master. Elisha said to him, "Where did you go, Gehazi?"

And he said, "Your servant did not go anywhere."

26 Then he said to him, "Did not my heart go with you when the man turned back from his chariot to meet you? Is it time to receive money and to receive clothing, olive groves and vineyards, sheep and oxen, male and female servants?

27 Therefore the leprosy of Naaman shall cling to you and your descendants forever." And he went out from his presence leprous, as white as snow.

Summary

After being healed by the prophet Elisha, who refused his gifts, Naaman, the commander of the army of Syria, sets out to return to his country with his entire delegation. Gehazi, Elisha's servant, pursues him secretly until he catches up. There he tells him that Elisha asks him to send a talent of silver and two changes of clothes for two of the sons of the prophets who have just arrived at his house. Promptly, Naaman gave him the clothes and even urged him to accept double the amount of money. Gehazi hid them in his home before returning to Elisha. When the prophet asks him where he was, he lies and says he didn't go anywhere. Elisha reveals to him what he has done and informs him that, as punishment, Naaman's leprosy will fall on him and all his descendants forever. Gehazi leaves the presence of Elisha, stricken with leprosy, as a reward for his greed and deception.

This passage shows the consequences of dishonesty as well as the importance of integrity and obedience in the eyes of God.

2 Kings 12:4-16

4 And Jehoash said to the priests, "All the money of the dedicated gifts that are brought into the house of the Lord—each man's census

money, each man's assessment money—and all the money that a man purposes in his heart to bring into the house of the Lord,

5 let the priests take it themselves, each from his constituency; and let them repair the damages of the temple, wherever any dilapidation is found."

6 Now it was so, by the twenty-third year of King Jehoash, that the priests had not repaired the damages of the temple.

7 So King Jehoash called Jehoiada the priest and the other priests, and said to them, "Why have you not repaired the damages of the temple? Now therefore, do not take more money from your constituency, but deliver it for repairing the damages of the temple."

8 And the priests agreed that they would neither receive more money from the people, nor repair the damages of the temple.

9 Then Jehoiada the priest took a chest, bored a hole in its lid, and set it beside the altar, on the right side as one comes into the house of the Lord; and the priests who kept the door put there all the money brought into the house of the Lord.

10 So it was, whenever they saw that there was much money in the chest, that the king's scribe and the high priest came up and put it in bags, and counted the money that was found in the house of the Lord.

11 Then they gave the money, which had been apportioned, into the hands of those who did the work, who had the oversight of the house of the Lord; and they paid it out to the carpenters and builders who worked on the house of the Lord,

12 and to masons and stonecutters, and for buying timber and hewn stone, to repair the damage of the house of the Lord, and for all that was paid out to repair the temple.

13 However there were not made for the house of the Lord basins of silver, trimmers, sprinkling-bowls, trumpets, any articles of gold or articles of silver, from the money brought into the house of the Lord.

14 But they gave that to the workmen, and they repaired the house of the Lord with it.

15 Moreover they did not require an account from the men into whose hand they delivered the money to be paid to workmen, for they dealt faithfully.

16 The money from the trespass offerings and the money from the sin offerings was not brought into the house of the Lord. It belonged to the priests.

Summary

Joash, king of Judah, takes the initiative to launch a project to renovate the house of the Lord. To do this, he calls the priests to collect, each in his district, money from the people to repair everything that needs to be repaired in the temple. He told them that only funds intended for the maintenance of the temple should be used for this purpose.

In the twenty-third year of his reign, King Joash noticed that no repairs had been carried out in the temple by the priests. He then calls Jehoiada the priest and the other priests and asks them why the renovation work has never begun. No answer to this question was provided.

During this meeting with the king, they agree to:

- no longer collect people's money
- place a chest, with a hole in its lid, next to the altar to collect all the money intended for the temple restoration project
- call the king's secretary, when the chest is full, who will come and count the money and then give it to those who are in charge of the work
- entrust the work to a third party
- supervise the completion of restoration work

This passage highlights King Joash's commitment to restoring God's temple and the importance of faithful stewardship in the maintenance of sacred sites within the Kingdom of Judah.

2 Kings 15:19-20

19 Pul king of Assyria came against the land; and Menahem gave Pul a thousand talents of silver, that his hand might be with him to strengthen the kingdom under his control.

20 And Menahem exacted the money from Israel, from all the very wealthy, from each man fifty shekels of silver, to give to the king of Assyria. So the king of Assyria turned back, and did not stay there in the land.

Summary

In this text, we find Pul, king of Assyria, who invades the land of Israel. Menahem, who became king of Israel by conspiracy, undertakes to pay him tribute in order to remain in power and consolidate his position. To achieve this, he imposes a special tax on everyone who has money—in other words, those who are rich in the country—in order to give this money to the king of Assyria. Thus, he imposes on everyone the payment of fifty shekels of silver in order to be able to collect a thousand talents of silver on behalf of the king of Assyria.

This passage highlights the precarious political situation in Israel at the time. It also highlights Menachem's pragmatic approach to dealing with the threat posed by Assyria.

2 Kings 22:7-9

7 However there need be no accounting made with them of the money delivered into their hand, because they deal faithfully."

8 Then Hilkiah the high priest said to Shaphan the scribe, "I have found the Book of the Law in the house of the Lord." And Hilkiah gave the book to Shaphan, and he read it.

9 So Shaphan the scribe went to the king, bringing the king word, saying, "Your servants have gathered the money that was found in the house, and have delivered it into the hand of those who do the work, who oversee the house of the Lord."

Summary

In the eighteenth year of the reign of Josiah, king of Judah, he sent his secretary, Shaphan, to meet the High Priest, Hilkiah, to ask him to collect money to renovate the house of the Lord. The money collected is given to those responsible for the work. It was not considered appropriate to hold them accountable since they are recognized as honest. However, during the work, Hilkiah finds the book of the law in the temple and gives it to Shaphan, who takes the time to read it. When presenting his report on the progress of the work to the king, Shaphan tells him about the book found in the temple and reads it to him.

2 Kings 23:34-35

34 Then Pharaoh Necho made Eliakim the son of Josiah king in place of his father Josiah, and changed his name to Jehoiakim. And Pharaoh took Jehoahaz and went to Egypt, and he died there.

35 So Jehoiakim gave the silver and gold to Pharaoh; but he taxed the land to give money according to the command of Pharaoh; he exacted the silver and gold from the people of the land, from every one according to his assessment, to give it to Pharaoh Necho.

Summary

After taking King Jehoahaz prisoner, Pharaoh Neco established Eliakim as king of Judah in his place. He changes his name to Jehoiakim and requires him to pay a heavy tribute. Under the orders of the Pharaoh, he sets up a tax and determines the amount that everyone must pay in order to be able to collect the money to give to the Pharaoh.

Chapter 8
Money in the Book of 2 Chronicles

2 Chronicles 24:4-14

4 Now it happened after this that Joash set his heart on repairing the house of the Lord.

5 Then he gathered the priests and the Levites, and said to them, "Go out to the cities of Judah, and gather from all Israel money to repair the house of your God from year to year, and see that you do it quickly."

However the Levites did not do it quickly.

6 So the king called Jehoiada the chief priest, and said to him, "Why have you not required the Levites to bring in from Judah and from Jerusalem the collection, according to the commandment of Moses the servant of the Lord and of the assembly of Israel, for the tabernacle of witness?"

7 For the sons of Athaliah, that wicked woman, had broken into the house of God, and had also presented all the dedicated things of the house of the Lord to the Baals.

8 Then at the king's command they made a chest, and set it outside at the gate of the house of the Lord.

9 And they made a proclamation throughout Judah and Jerusalem to bring to the Lord the collection that Moses the servant of God had imposed on Israel in the wilderness.

10 Then all the leaders and all the people rejoiced, brought their contributions, and put them into the chest until all had given.

11 So it was, at that time, when the chest was brought to the king's official by the hand of the Levites, and when they saw that there was much money, that the king's scribe and the high priest's officer came and emptied the chest, and took it and returned it to its place. Thus they did day by day, and gathered money in abundance.

12 The king and Jehoiada gave it to those who did the work of the service of the house of the Lord; and they hired masons and carpenters to repair the house of the Lord, and also those who worked in iron and bronze to restore the house of the Lord.

13 So the workmen labored, and the work was completed by them; they restored the house of God to its original condition and reinforced it.

14 When they had finished, they brought the rest of the money before the king and Jehoiada; they made from it articles for the house of the Lord, articles for serving and offering, spoons and vessels of gold and silver. And they offered burnt offerings in the house of the Lord continually all the days of Jehoiada.

Summary

King Joash wants to repair the temple in Jerusalem. He gathered the priests and the Levites and asked them to go through the cities of the kingdom to collect money from the people to carry out the work. Despite King Josiah's order to act with haste, the Levites did not act promptly. The king called the high priest, Jehoiada, to inquire about the reason for the delay, but none could be given. The king therefore ordered a chest to be placed at the entrance to the temple, and a decree was published throughout the country asking the people to bring in the tax that had been put in place by Moses. The chiefs and all the people rejoiced at the initiative and reacted promptly by providing all the money they had to pay. Once filled, the Levites handed over the chest to the king's inspectors, where the king's secretary and the high priest's commissioner took care of emptying it and then replacing it at the entrance to the temple. They did this process on a daily basis because the money collected flowed in abundance. This money, thus collected, is given to the team in charge of the renovation work. At the end, the temple returned to its former glory as the pride of the people, ensuring the continuation of worship and sacrifice according to the law of Moses.

This passage underlines the importance of the temple in the religious life of Judah and highlights the commitment of King Joash as well as the enthusiasm of the people for its restoration.

2 Chronicles 34:8-18

8 In the eighteenth year of his reign, when he had purged the land and the temple, he sent Shaphan the son of Azaliah, Maaseiah the governor of the city, and Joah the son of Joahaz the recorder, to repair the house of the Lord his God.

9 When they came to Hilkiah the high priest, they delivered the money that was brought into the house of God, which the Levites who kept the doors had gathered from the hand of Manasseh and Ephraim, from all the remnant of Israel, from all Judah and Benjamin, and which they had brought back to Jerusalem.

10 Then they put it in the hand of the foremen who had the oversight of the house of the Lord; and they gave it to the workmen who worked in the house of the Lord, to repair and restore the house.

11 They gave it to the craftsmen and builders to buy hewn stone and timber for beams, and to floor the houses which the kings of Judah had destroyed.

12 And the men did the work faithfully. Their overseers were Jahath and Obadiah the Levites, of the sons of Merari, and Zechariah and Meshullam, of the sons of the Kohathites, to supervise. Others of the Levites, all of whom were skillful with instruments of music,

13 were over the burden bearers and were overseers of all who did work in any kind of service. And some of the Levites were scribes, officers, and gatekeepers.

14 Now when they brought out the money that was brought into the house of the Lord, Hilkiah the priest found the Book of the Law of the Lord given by Moses.

15 Then Hilkiah answered and said to Shaphan the scribe, "I have found the Book of the Law in the house of the Lord." And Hilkiah gave the book to Shaphan.

16 So Shaphan carried the book to the king, bringing the king word, saying, "All that was committed to your servants they are doing.

17 And they have gathered the money that was found in the house of the Lord, and have delivered it into the hand of the overseers and the workmen."

18 Then Shaphan the scribe told the king, saying, "Hilkiah the priest has given me a book." And Shaphan read it before the king.

Summary

After purifying the land and the temple, King Josiah undertook, in the eighteenth year of his reign, the project of restoring the house of God. To carry out this project, money was collected from all of Israel and all of Judah by the Levites and then given into the hands of those who were responsible for the renovation work. For their part, they distribute the money to artisans and workers who carry out the repairs, including carpenters and masons. During the work, Hilkiah, the high priest, found the book of the Law of Moses in the temple and gave it to Shaphan, the scribe. While reporting to the king on the progress of the work, Shaphan told him about the book of the law that had been found and read its contents to King Josiah, who was very touched by what he heard.

Chapter 9
Money in the Book of Ezra

Ezra 3: 6-7

6 From the first day of the seventh month they began to offer burnt offerings to the Lord, although the foundation of the temple of the Lord had not been laid.

7 They also gave money to the masons and the carpenters, and food, drink, and oil to the people of Sidon and Tyre to bring cedar logs from Lebanon to the sea, to Joppa, according to the permission which they had from Cyrus king of Persia.

Summary

Coming from Babylon to rebuild the temple at the request of Cyrus, king of Persia, the people of Israel gathered in Jerusalem as one man. While the foundations of the temple were not yet built, they reestablished the altar of God so that they could offer their morning and evening sacrifices. For the construction of the temple, money was collected and given to the stonecutters and carpenters, while food, oil, and drinks were collected and given to the Sidonians and Tyrians to bring back wood cedar from Lebanon.

This passage highlights the commitment of the Israelites to restore the temple, worship, and sacrifices in Jerusalem according to what the law of Moses prescribes.

Ezra 7:14-18

14 And whereas you are being sent by the king and his seven counselors to inquire concerning Judah and Jerusalem, with regard to the Law of your God which is in your hand;

15 and whereas you are to carry the silver and gold which the king and his counselors have freely offered to the God of Israel, whose dwelling is in Jerusalem;

16 and whereas all the silver and gold that you may find in all the province of Babylon, along with the freewill offering of the people and the priests, are to be freely offered for the house of their God in Jerusalem—

17 now therefore, be careful to buy with this money bulls, rams, and lambs, with their grain offerings and their drink offerings, and offer them on the altar of the house of your God in Jerusalem.

18 And whatever seems good to you and your brethren to do with the rest of the silver and the gold, do it according to the will of your God.

Summary

The king of Persia, Artaxerxes, published and delivered to Ezra a decree declaring to let go to Jerusalem all the people of Israel, priests, and Levites in the kingdom who wish to leave. This decree gives him the right, through the king and his seven advisors, to inspect Judah and Jerusalem with regard to the law of God and to carry the substantial gifts in gold and silver that the king and his advisors offer to God, as well as the voluntary donations made by the people and the priests for the temple of God in Jerusalem. He also received the mandate to purchase with the money collected everything necessary for the offerings and sacrifices and to present them on the altar of the temple in Jerusalem.

This passage shows the support and favor that God gave to Ezra in his efforts to restore worship and obedience to the law among the Israelites.

Chapter 10
Money in the Book of Nehemiah

Nehemiah 5: 1-5

1 And there was a great outcry of the people and their wives against their Jewish brethren.

2 For there were those who said, "We, our sons, and our daughters are many; therefore let us get grain, that we may eat and live."

3 There were also some who said, "We have mortgaged our lands and vineyards and houses, that we might buy grain because of the famine."

4 There were also those who said, "We have borrowed money for the king's tax on our lands and vineyards.

5 Yet now our flesh is as the flesh of our brethren, our children as their children; and indeed we are forcing our sons and our daughters to be slaves, and some of our daughters have been brought into slavery. It is not in our power to redeem them, for other men have our lands and vineyards."

Summary

As the construction of the wall progressed under threat from enemies surrounding the territory of Judah, were among the people raised their voices to protest against the social injustice imposed on them. Indeed, to protect themselves against the incessant threats of their enemies, the people had to work with one hand and hold their weapons with the other in addition to alternating between construction work during the day and surveillance at night; despite this, they had to meet tax requirements as well as their commitments to their creditors. Faced with this injustice, they rise up to protest. Among their demands were:

- Starvation
- Taxes
- Mortgages
- Borrowings

They complain about:

- magistrates who, even despite particular circumstances, continue to demand taxes from them
- nobles who make them mortgage their houses, their fields and their vineyards or borrow money from them at interest

No longer able to bear the injustice, the people openly raised their voices to protest against the nobles and magistrates.

Nehemiah 5:7-12

7 After serious thought, I rebuked the nobles and rulers, and said to them, "Each of you is exacting usury from his brother." So I called a great assembly against them.

8 And I said to them, "According to our ability we have redeemed our Jewish brethren who were sold to the nations. Now indeed, will you even sell your brethren? Or should they be sold to us?"

Then they were silenced and found nothing to say.

9 Then I said, "What you are doing is not good. Should you not walk in the fear of our God because of the reproach of the nations, our enemies?

10 I also, with my brethren and my servants, am lending them money and grain. Please, let us stop this usury!

11 Restore now to them, even this day, their lands, their vineyards, their olive groves, and their houses, also a hundredth of the money and the grain, the new wine and the oil, that you have charged them."

12 So they said, "We will restore it, and will require nothing from them; we will do as you say."

Then I called the priests, and required an oath from them that they would do according to this promise.

Summary

In this passage, Nehemiah responds to the people's outcry regarding the economic injustices occurring within the community.

He organizes a public gathering where he confronts the nobles and officials in the presence of the people on issues of social injustice that concern the community. He openly reprimands them for exploiting and taking advantage of the community by charging interest on money loans and maintaining taxes, which adds additional burdens to their own Jewish brothers. He demands that they return to the people everything they took as collateral (fields, vineyards, olive trees, and houses) as well as one-hundredth of the money, wheat, and oil that they had demanded as interest. Without complaining, the nobles and magistrates accepted Nehemiah's demands, which made them swear, in the presence of the priests, to respect their word. The whole assembly agrees and begins to praise God.

This text highlights Nehemiah's leadership, commitment, and concrete actions toward social justice within the community.

Chapter 11
Money in the Book of Esther

Esther 4:3-8

3 And in every province where the king's command and decree arrived, there was great mourning among the Jews, with fasting, weeping, and wailing; and many lay in sackcloth and ashes.

4 So Esther's maids and eunuchs came and told her, and the queen was deeply distressed. Then she sent garments to clothe Mordecai and take his sackcloth away from him, but he would not accept them.

5 Then Esther called Hathach, one of the king's eunuchs whom he had appointed to attend her, and she gave him a command concerning Mordecai, to learn what and why this was.

6 So Hathach went out to Mordecai in the city square that was in front of the king's gate.

7 And Mordecai told him all that had happened to him, and the sum of money that Haman had promised to pay into the king's treasuries to destroy the Jews.

8 He also gave him a copy of the written decree for their destruction, which was given at Shushan, that he might show it to Esther and explain it to her, and that he might command her to go in to the king to make supplication to him and plead before him for her people.

MONEY IN THE BIBLE

Summary

After learning of Haman's plot to kill all the Jews in the Persian Empire and seeing the decree issued by the king to this effect, Mordecai plunged into lamentation and mourning, tearing his clothes, putting on sackcloth and ashes, and shouting in the streets of Susa.

At the same time, Jews across the country joined in prayer, fasting, and mourning. Having learned of Mordecai's distress, Queen Esther sends him clothes to replace his sacks, but he refuses them. He then told the messenger everything that had happened to him and revealed the amount of money that Haman had promised to deliver to the King's Treasury following the massacre of the Jews. He sends to Queen Esther the decree orchestrated by Haman to exterminate the Jews and asks her to intercede with the king on behalf of the people of Israel.

Chapter 12
Money in the Book of Job

Job 31:35-40

35 Oh, that I had one to hear me! Here is my mark. Oh, that the Almighty would answer me, That my Prosecutor had written a book!

36 Surely I would carry it on my shoulder, And bind it on me like a crown;

37 I would declare to Him the number of my steps; Like a prince I would approach Him.

38 "If my land cries out against me, And its furrows weep together;

39 If I have eaten its fruit without money, Or caused its owners to lose their lives;

40 Then let thistles grow instead of wheat, And weeds instead of barley."

Summary

In this text, we find Job pleading his innocence before God. Insisting that God answer him, he questions what he is accused of. He promises to strap the indictment on his shoulder and wear it on his forehead. Confident that he has nothing to reproach himself for, Job asks to confront his accuser about everything he is accused of. He even went so far as to declare that if he ate the fruits of his own land without money or if he murdered someone to steal their land, let the earth produce thorns for him as punishment in place of wheat and tares in place of barley. Job is willing to accept any deserved punishment in response to any wrongdoing he may have committed.

This passage reflects Job's unwavering belief in his own innocence, even in the midst of deep suffering and despair.

Job 42:9-11

9 So Eliphaz the Temanite and Bildad the Shuhite and Zophar the Naamathite went, and did according as the Lord commanded them: the Lord also accepted Job.

10 And the Lord turned the captivity of Job, when he prayed for his friends: also the Lord gave Job twice as much as he had before.

11 Then came there unto him all his brethren, and all his sisters, and all they that had been of his acquaintance before, and did eat bread with him in his house: and they bemoaned him, and comforted him over all the evil that the Lord had brought upon him: every man also gave him a piece of money, and every one an earring of gold.

Summary

In this passage, God rebukes Job's friends, Eliphaz the Temanite, Bildad the Shuhite, and Zophar the Naamathite, for not speaking righteously about Him as Job did. Then He asks them to go to Job to present a sacrifice and for Job to pray for their forgiveness. God receives Job's prayer, restores him to his original state, and blesses him by doubling his wealth. All those who had fled from Job returned to comfort him, to eat with him, and to bring him money and gold.

Chapter 13
Money in the Book of Psalms

Psalms 15:1-5

1 Lord, who may abide in Your tabernacle? Who may dwell in Your holy hill?

2 He who walks uprightly, And works righteousness, And speaks the truth in his heart;

3 He who does not backbite with his tongue, Nor does evil to his neighbor, Nor does he take up a reproach against his friend;

4 In whose eyes a vile person is despised, But he honors those who fear the Lord; He who swears to his own hurt and does not change;

5 He who does not put out his money at usury, Nor does he take a bribe against the innocent. He who does these things shall never be moved.

Summary

In his meditation, David asks God two questions that can be reduced to one: who can dwell in the presence of God? In answering this question, David gives us the characteristics of such a man. It's someone who:

- walks in integrity
- practices justice
- tells the truth
- does not slander

- does not harm his neighbor
- does not reproach his neighbor
- despises the contemptible
- honors those who fear God
- keeps its commitments,
- does not lend his money at interest
- is not corrupted

David concludes by saying that such a person would be unshakable.

Chapter 14
Money in the Book of Proverbs

Proverbs 7:6-20

6 For at the window of my house I looked through my lattice,

7 And saw among the simple, I perceived among the youths, A young man devoid of understanding,

8 Passing along the street near her corner; And he took the path to her house

9 In the twilight, in the evening, In the black and dark night.

10 And there a woman met him, With the attire of a harlot, and a crafty heart.

11 She was loud and rebellious, Her feet would not stay at home.

12 At times she was outside, at times in the open square, Lurking at every corner.

13 So she caught him and kissed him; With an impudent face she said to him:

14 "I have peace offerings with me; Today I have paid my vows.

15 So I came out to meet you, Diligently to seek your face, And I have found you.

16 I have spread my bed with tapestry, Colored coverings of Egyptian linen.

17 I have perfumed my bed With myrrh, aloes, and cinnamon.

18 Come, let us take our fill of love until morning; Let us delight ourselves with love.

19 For my husband is not at home; He has gone on a long journey;

20 He has taken a bag of money with him, And will come home on the appointed day."

Summary

In this text, Solomon tells us about the tricks used by the wife of a rich man, presented by her behavior as a prostitute, to seduce a young man lacking discernment. While her husband has gone to a distant country, taking only a single bag of money and thinking of leaving her in the comfort of their home, she gets up, presents her sacrifices, prepares her room elegantly, and leaves her home looking for this young man whom she had a crush on for a while. After spending her time looking for him everywhere, she finally finds him at dusk as he returns home. Without any embarrassment, she grabs him and kisses him in the street without letting him say a word. She told him that her husband had gone far away and had enough money to stay gone for awhile, that she had presented her sacrifices, and that she had prepared and perfumed her room for him. In other words, all the conditions are met for her to give herself up to him and sleep with him. Without thinking and without saying a word, the young man follows her like a sheep being led to the slaughterhouse.

This passage serves as a warning, emphasizing the importance of wisdom and discernment, and shows how a lack of wisdom can lead to one's downfall.

Chapter 15
Money in the Book of Ecclesiastes

Ecclesiastes 7:11-12

11 Wisdom is good with an inheritance, And profitable to those who see the sun.

12 For wisdom is a defense as money is a defense, But the excellence of knowledge is that wisdom gives life to those who have it.

Summary

In this passage, Solomon emphasizes that wisdom goes well with an inheritance but that it is especially profitable for those who are alive to enjoy it. From there, he draws a parallel between wisdom and money. While both provide good protection to those who possess them, they differ in that wisdom gives life to those who have it, while money is a double-edged sword. And that gives an advantage to everyone who knows the difference.

This passage teaches us that instead of choosing between wisdom and money, it is profitable to have both. Indeed, money improves the effectiveness of wisdom while it reduces the harmful power of money. The combination between the two provides the holder with a joyful and well-balanced life.

Ecclesiastes 10:19

19 A feast is made for laughter, And wine makes merry; But money answers everything.

MONEY IN THE BIBLE

Summary

In this text, Solomon states that when we organize a feast, it is with the aim of making the guests laugh, while the aim of wine is to make people joyful. In other words, everything has a purpose. Likewise, money has a purpose, which is to be an answer to everything. This means that even when money is not the best solution to a problem, it will always be part of the list of possible solutions.

Chapter 16
Money in the Book of Isaiah

Isaiah 43:22-24

22 "But you have not called upon Me, O Jacob; And you have been weary of Me, O Israel.

23 You have not brought Me the sheep for your burnt offerings, Nor have you honored Me with your sacrifices. I have not caused you to serve with grain offerings, Nor wearied you with incense.

24 You have bought Me no sweet cane with money, Nor have you satisfied Me with the fat of your sacrifices; But you have burdened Me with your sins, You have wearied Me with your iniquities.

Summary

Through the mouth of Isaiah, God reproaches the people of Israel for their ingratitude and their unfaithfulness toward Him. He reprimands them for:

- not having invoked Him
- having abandoned Him by turning to other gods
- not honoring Him by offering Him sacrifices
- not having used their money to buy Him perfumes
- having tired Him with their iniquities

At the same time, God reminds them that He never tormented them for offerings.

This passage reminds us that it is important to show gratitude to God, honor His faithfulness, and not hesitate to use our money to do so.

Isaiah 52:1-3

1 Awake, awake! Put on your strength, O Zion; Put on your beautiful garments, O Jerusalem, the holy city! For the uncircumcised and the unclean Shall no longer come to you.

2 Shake yourself from the dust, arise; Sit down, O Jerusalem! Loose yourself from the bonds of your neck, O captive daughter of Zion!

3 For thus says the Lord: "You have sold yourselves for nothing, And you shall be redeemed without money."

Summary

In this passage, God invites, through the prophet Isaiah, Jerusalem to wake up and dress in her most beautiful clothes, announcing to her that the uncircumcised and the impure will no longer enter their territory. God invites Jerusalem to shake off the dust on her, dress up nicely, and remove her bonds of captivity. He tells them that just as their captivity was accomplished without money, their redemption will also be accomplished without money.

This passage announces the end of the captivity and oppression of Jerusalem by its enemy countries. It also announces the restoration of Jerusalem, which will recover its identity and its glory through the sovereign authority of God.

Isaiah 55:1-3

1 "Ho! Everyone who thirsts, Come to the waters; And you who have no money, Come, buy and eat. Yes, come, buy wine and milk without money and without price.

2 Why do you spend money for what is not bread, And your wages for what does not satisfy? Listen carefully to Me, and eat what is good, And let your soul delight itself in abundance.

3 Incline your ear, and come to Me. Hear, and your soul shall live; And I will make an everlasting covenant with you—The sure mercies of David.

Summary

In this text, the prophet calls all those who are hungry and thirsty to come and eat and drink and buy wine and milk without paying anything. He exhorts them to listen attentively to God's invitation and come to Him, promising that those who do so will find salvation for their souls.

Chapter 17
Money in the Book of Jeremiah

Jeremiah 32:8-14

8 Then Hanamel my uncle's son came to me in the court of the prison according to the word of the Lord, and said to me, 'Please buy my field that is in Anathoth, which is in the country of Benjamin; for the right of inheritance is yours, and the redemption yours; buy it for yourself.' Then I knew that this was the word of the Lord.

9 So I bought the field from Hanamel, the son of my uncle who was in Anathoth, and weighed out to him the money—seventeen shekels of silver.

10 And I signed the deed and sealed it, took witnesses, and weighed the money on the scales.

11 So I took the purchase deed, both that which was sealed according to the law and custom, and that which was open;

12 and I gave the purchase deed to Baruch the son of Neriah, son of Mahseiah, in the presence of Hanamel my uncle's son, and in the presence of the witnesses who signed the purchase deed, before all the Jews who sat in the court of the prison.

13 "Then I charged Baruch before them, saying,

14 'Thus says the Lord of hosts, the God of Israel: "Take these deeds, both this purchase deed which is sealed and this deed which is open, and put them in an earthen vessel, that they may last many days."

Summary

While Jeremiah is in prison, God informs him that Hanameel, son of his uncle Shallum, will offer to acquire a field in Anathoth, in the land of Benjamin, for which he has the right of redemption. As the Lord had told him, Hanameel came to see him while he was standing in the courtyard of the prison and offered to buy the field for which he is heir and has right of redemption. Without hesitation, the prophet Jeremiah accepts and the cost of the operation amounts to seventeen shekels of silver. The money is paid in full for the field, and the transaction is concluded by a deed of sale signed in the presence of witnesses. This act symbolizes the return to normalcy and prosperity after the period of exile and destruction.

Jeremiah 32:24-28

24 'Look, the siege mounds! They have come to the city to take it; and the city has been given into the hand of the Chaldeans who fight against it, because of the sword and famine and pestilence. What You have spoken has happened; there You see it!

25 And You have said to me, O Lord God, "Buy the field for money, and take witnesses"!—yet the city has been given into the hand of the Chaldeans.' "

26 Then the word of the Lord came to Jeremiah, saying,

27 "Behold, I am the Lord, the God of all flesh. Is there anything too hard for Me?

28 Therefore thus says the Lord: 'Behold, I will give this city into the hand of the Chaldeans, into the hand of Nebuchadnezzar king of Babylon, and he shall take it.

Summary

Following the acquisition of the field from the hands of Hanameel, Jeremiah addresses a prayer to God to express his astonishment and his incomprehension. Indeed, God ordered him to acquire with money a field in a context where the city of Jerusalem was besieged by the Babylonians who were preparing to enter it, destroy it, and then take the people into captivity. In other words, the prophet Jeremiah wants to tell God that the acquisition of the field seems inappropriate or even useless. In response, God reassures Jeremiah by recalling that with Him, nothing is surprising. Then He reaffirms to Jeremiah that the city will indeed be destroyed because of the sins of the children of Israel and that the people will be taken into captivity. He further confides that when the time comes, he will bring back the people of Babylon and restore the land.

Jeremiah 32:42-44

42 "For thus says the Lord: 'Just as I have brought all this great calamity on this people, so I will bring on them all the good that I have promised them.

43 And fields will be bought in this land of which you say, "It is desolate, without man or beast; it has been given into the hand of the Chaldeans."

44 Men will buy fields for money, sign deeds and seal them, and take witnesses, in the land of Benjamin, in the places around Jerusalem, in the cities of Judah, in the cities of the mountains, in the cities of the lowland, and in the cities of the South; for I will cause their captives to return,' says the Lord."

Summary

In this passage, God reaffirms to Jeremiah that as He brought calamities upon the land, so He will bring upon the people all the good things He has promised. He will bring back the people from captivity, and this desert, described by Jeremiah as without men or beasts, which is delivered into the hands of the Chaldeans, will be transformed into fertile fields that will be bought for money with sales contracts signed in the presence of witnesses. This will happen everywhere in the country—in the plains, in the cities, and in the mountains—when the people return from captivity.

Chapter 18
Money in the Book of Lamentations

Lamentations 5:1-5

1 Remember, O Lord, what is come upon us: consider, and behold our reproach.

2 Our inheritance is turned to strangers, our houses to aliens.

3 We are orphans and fatherless, our mothers are as widows.

4 We have drunken our water for money; our wood is sold unto us.

5 Our necks are under persecution: we labour, and have no rest.

Summary

In this passage, faced with the desolation and distress of the people of Judah following the destruction of Jerusalem, the Prophet raises his voice to cry out to God. In his prayer, he describes the misery, suffering, and despair that are everywhere, both on faces and on the landscape. There is no more pride, no more glory, no more joy; the country is abandoned, without protection, like an orphan. The Prophet says that water and firewood must be acquired at a price of money. The people must turn to foreign countries like Egypt or Assyria for food at the risk of their lives. He asks God not to forget or abandon them and to restore the nation.

Chapter 19
Money in the Book of Micah

Micah 3:8-12

8 But truly I am full of power by the Spirit of the Lord, And of justice and might, To declare to Jacob his transgression And to Israel his sin.

9 Now hear this, You heads of the house of Jacob And rulers of the house of Israel, Who abhor justice And pervert all equity,

10 Who build up Zion with bloodshed And Jerusalem with iniquity:

11 Her heads judge for a bribe, Her priests teach for pay, And her prophets divine for money. Yet they lean on the Lord, and say, "Is not the Lord among us? No harm can come upon us."

12 Therefore because of you Zion shall be plowed like a field, Jerusalem shall become heaps of ruins, And the mountain of the temple Like the bare hills of the forest.

Summary

In this passage, the prophet Micah addresses the leaders of Israel who were to care for the people and serve as an example to them. On the contrary, they abuse, take advantage of, tear off, and devour the flesh of the people. In this text, the prophet Micah raises his voice and rebukes their behavior. He presents them as people who:

— Hate justice
— Pervert all that is right

- Built with blood
- Judge for gifts
- Have priests who teach for a salary
- Have prophets who predict for money

He tells them that, because of them, misfortune will come to the country. So:

- Zion will be plowed like a field.
- Jerusalem will become a heap of stones.
- The temple mountain will transform into a peak covered in wood.

Chapter 20
Money in the Book of Matthew

Matthew 17:24-27

24 When they had come to Capernaum, those who received the temple tax came to Peter and said, "Does your Teacher not pay the temple tax?"

25 He said, "Yes." And when he had come into the house, Jesus anticipated him, saying, "What do you think, Simon? From whom do the kings of the earth take customs or taxes, from their sons or from strangers?"

26 Peter said to Him, "From strangers." Jesus said to him, "Then the sons are free.

27 Nevertheless, lest we offend them, go to the sea, cast in a hook, and take the fish that comes up first. And when you have opened its mouth, you will find a piece of money; take that and give it to them for Me and you."

Summary

Tax collectors from the city of Capernaum come to confirm with Peter that Jesus pays the taxes owed to the temple. Without hesitation, Peter responds to them with affirmation. Once they arrive at their destination, and before Peter comes to approach him on the subject, Jesus asks him if these taxes must be paid by citizens or by foreigners. Peter confirms that citizens are exempt and that only foreigners must pay these taxes. After agreeing with him that citizens are exempt, Jesus tells Peter to go fish and, in the mouth of the first fish he catches, he will find money to pay the taxes for both of them.

In this passage, Jesus takes advantage of a seemingly innocuous situation to teach us a fundamental lesson in the process of creating wealth, namely that money is available everywhere, even in the mouth of a fish, which is the most unexpected place to find money.

Matthew 22:17-22

17 Tell us, therefore, what do You think? Is it lawful to pay taxes to Caesar, or not?"

18 But Jesus perceived their wickedness, and said, "Why do you test Me, you hypocrites?

19 Show Me the tax money." So they brought Him a denarius.

20 And He said to them, "Whose image and inscription is this?"

21 They said to Him, "Caesar's." And He said to them, "Render therefore to Caesar the things that are Caesar's, and to God the things that are God's."

22 When they had heard these words, they marveled, and left Him and went their way.

Summary

The Pharisees plan to trap Jesus through his own words. To do this, they sent their disciples to him, accompanied by the Herodians, to question him about the legitimacy of paying taxes to Caesar. Knowing what they were thinking, Jesus responded by asking them to present him with a denarius. When the last one is presented to him, he asks them whose effigy and inscription it is. To this question, they answer that they are both from Caesar. Then Jesus gives them this response that has become so famous: "Render therefore to Caesar the things that are Caesar's, and to God the things that are God's." With this response, Jesus neither denies nor affirms the payment of taxes, but he teaches the principle of giving to earthly authorities what is rightfully theirs while recognizing the superior authority of God. Jesus' wise response surprises and leaves the Pharisees and Herodians stunned and unable to continue their mission to trap Jesus in his words.

Matthew 25:14-30

14 "For the kingdom of heaven is like a man traveling to a far country, who called his own servants and delivered his goods to them.

15 And to one he gave five talents, to another two, and to another one, to each according to his own ability; and immediately he went on a journey.

16 Then he who had received the five talents went and traded with them, and made another five talents.

17 And likewise he who had received two gained two more also.

18 But he who had received one went and dug in the ground, and hid his lord's money.

19 After a long time the lord of those servants came and settled accounts with them.

20 "So he who had received five talents came and brought five other talents, saying, 'Lord, you delivered to me five talents; look, I have gained five more talents besides them.'

21 His lord said to him, 'Well done, good and faithful servant; you were faithful over a few things, I will make you ruler over many things. Enter into the joy of your lord.'

22 He also who had received two talents came and said, 'Lord, you delivered to me two talents; look, I have gained two more talents besides them.'

23 His lord said to him, 'Well done, good and faithful servant; you have been faithful over a few things, I will make you ruler over many things. Enter into the joy of your lord.'

24 "Then he who had received the one talent came and said, 'Lord, I knew you to be a hard man, reaping where you have not sown, and gathering where you have not scattered seed.

25 And I was afraid, and went and hid your talent in the ground. Look, there you have what is yours.'

26 "But his lord answered and said to him, 'You wicked and lazy servant, you knew that I reap where I have not sown, and gather where I have not scattered seed.

27 So you ought to have deposited my money with the bankers, and at my coming I would have received back my own with interest.

28 So take the talent from him, and give it to him who has ten talents.

29 'For to everyone who has, more will be given, and he will have abundance; but from him who does not have, even what he has will be taken away.

30 And cast the unprofitable servant into the outer darkness. There will be weeping and gnashing of teeth.'

Summary

In this text, Jesus communicates a teaching through a parable commonly called the parable of the talents. This parable is about a master going on a journey who entrusts all his wealth, consisting solely of money, to his servants. Among his servants, three are highlighted in the text. Thus, he distributes five talents of silver to one servant, two talents to the second, and one talent to the third servant, each according to his management abilities. The first two servants invest and double the money entrusted to them, while the third servant buries his money in the ground out of fear of his master and does not invest it.

When he returns a long time later, the master invites his servants to come and present their management report to him. He congratulates the first two servants for their loyalty, their initiative, and their management. He rewards them by giving them much greater responsibilities and inviting them to share his joy. The third servant is punished and thrown into outer darkness for his laziness, his lack of initiative, and for not having invested the money received, which, in the end, was taken from him.

This parable teaches us that:

- God has given each person one or more gifts.
- God expects us to put our gifts to good use.
- God expects a return on the gifts He has placed in us.
- Rewards are reserved for those who manage their donations well.
- Punishments await those who waste their gifts.
- God encourages us to be entrepreneurs.
- We must develop and maintain a winning mentality.
- Money placed in the bank is the least profitable investment.

Matthew 28:11-15

11 Now while they were going, behold, some of the guard came into the city and reported to the chief priests all the things that had happened.

12 When they had assembled with the elders and consulted together, they gave a large sum of money to the soldiers,

13 saying, "Tell them, 'His disciples came at night and stole Him away while we slept.'

14 And if this comes to the governor's ears, we will appease him and make you secure."

15 So they took the money and did as they were instructed; and this saying is commonly reported among the Jews until this day.

Summary

While the women visiting Jesus' tomb were on their way to tell the disciples about his resurrection, some of the soldiers guarding the tomb entered the city to report to the chief priests everything that had happened and to inform them of the resurrection of Jesus. Following this report, the chief priests met with the elders and, together, they decided to bribe the soldiers by giving them a large sum of money. In exchange, they ask them to spread the news that the disciples came to steal Jesus' body while they were sleeping. Furthermore, they assured the soldiers that if this report reached the governor, they would satisfy him and ensure that they did not get into trouble. Taking these guarantees into consideration, the soldiers took the money and did what was asked of them.

This passage highlights the efforts made by religious authorities to hide the truth about the resurrection of Jesus. Despite their efforts, the truth about his resurrection could not be contained. However, this story has still circulated among Jews to this day.

Chapter 21
Money in the Book of Mark

Mark 6:7-9

7 And He called the twelve to Himself, and began to send them out two by two, and gave them power over unclean spirits.

8 He commanded them to take nothing for the journey except a staff—no bag, no bread, no copper in their money belts—

9 but to wear sandals, and not to put on two tunics.

Summary

In this text, Jesus calls the twelve disciples and sends them in pairs on a missionary journey. It gives them authority over unclean spirits, which can translate into the power to cast out demons and heal the sick. For this trip, he orders them not to take anything, not to take any luggage, neither bread, nor bags, nor money, nor two tunics, but a staff and sandals.

Mark 12:41-44

41 Now Jesus sat opposite the treasury and saw how the people put money into the treasury. And many who were rich put in much.

42 Then one poor widow came and threw in two mites, which make a quadrans.

43 So He called His disciples to Himself and said to them, "Assuredly, I say to you that this poor widow has put in more than all those who have given to the treasury;

44 for they all put in out of their abundance, but she out of her poverty put in all that she had, her whole livelihood."

Summary

This passage shows Jesus sitting in the temple and observing the people who come to leave their offerings. Among the people who came forward, not many wealthy people brought a lot of money. Then, a poor widow arrives who only had two coins to give, which represents one quadrans.

Thereupon, Jesus calls his disciples and tells them that the poor widow contributed more than all the rich people who gave a lot of money. He explains to them that the rich gave from their surplus, while the widow, from her poverty, put in everything she had, even everything she had to live on.

This passage emphasizes the value of sacrificial giving in that it is not the amount of the gift that matters but the heart and sacrifice behind the gift. The widow's offering was small in monetary terms, but it was a great sacrifice for her because it was all she had. This teaches us that God values our offerings not according to their monetary value but according to the spirit and good will with which they are given.

Mark 14:10-11

10 Then Judas Iscariot, one of the twelve, went to the chief priests to betray Him to them.

11 And when they heard it, they were glad, and promised to give him money. So he sought how he might conveniently betray Him.

Summary

Judas Iscariot, one of Jesus' twelve disciples, goes to see the chief priests with the aim of offering to deliver Jesus to them. Happy with such a proposal, the chief priests offer to give Judas Iscariot money in return, which he accepts. From that point, he works to find a favorable opportunity to deliver Jesus to them.

Chapter 22
Money in the Book of Luke

Luke 9: 1-3

1 Then He called His twelve disciples together and gave them power and authority over all demons, and to cure diseases.

2 He sent them to preach the kingdom of God and to heal the sick.

3 And He said to them, "Take nothing for the journey, neither staffs nor bag nor bread nor money; and do not have two tunics apiece."

Summary

In this text, Jesus gathers the twelve disciples, and after giving them authority and power to cast out demons and heal the sick, he sends them out to proclaim the kingdom of God and heal the sick. For this trip, he asks them not to take anything: no stick, no bag, no bread, no money, and not even an extra tunic.

Luke 19: 11-27

11 Now as they heard these things, He spoke another parable, because He was near Jerusalem and because they thought the kingdom of God would appear immediately.

12 Therefore He said: "A certain nobleman went into a far country to receive for himself a kingdom and to return.

13 So he called ten of his servants, delivered to them ten minas, and said to them, 'Do business till I come.'

14 But his citizens hated him, and sent a delegation after him, saying, 'We will not have this man to reign over us.'

15 "And so it was that when he returned, having received the kingdom, he then commanded these servants, to whom he had given the money, to be called to him, that he might know how much every man had gained by trading.

16 Then came the first, saying, 'Master, your mina has earned ten minas.'

17 And he said to him, 'Well done, good servant; because you were faithful in a very little, have authority over ten cities.'

18 And the second came, saying, 'Master, your mina has earned five minas.'

19 Likewise he said to him, 'You also be over five cities.'

20 "Then another came, saying, 'Master, here is your mina, which I have kept put away in a handkerchief.

21 For I feared you, because you are an austere man. You collect what you did not deposit, and reap what you did not sow.'

22 And he said to him, 'Out of your own mouth I will judge you, you wicked servant. You knew that I was an austere man, collecting what I did not deposit and reaping what I did not sow.

23 Why then did you not put my money in the bank, that at my coming I might have collected it with interest?'

24 "And he said to those who stood by, 'Take the mina from him, and give it to him who has ten minas.'

25 (But they said to him, 'Master, he has ten minas.')

26 'For I say to you, that to everyone who has will be given; and from him who does not have, even what he has will be taken away from him.

27 But bring here those enemies of mine, who did not want me to reign over them, and slay them before me.' "

Summary

While the Jews believed that the coming of God's kingdom was imminent, Jesus presents to them this parable where a nobleman goes to a distant land in order to receive a kingdom and return. Before leaving, he calls ten of his servants, distributes ten mina (monetary unit) to them, and asks them to do business with this money until his return.

After a while, the master returns. He summons his servants to present him with the management report on the money entrusted to them. Only three of the ten servants were able to submit a report. With the mina received, the first servant gained ten additional minas, the second gained five additional mines, while the third simply hid his mina and did not multiply it. As a reward, the first servant was placed in charge of ten cities, the second was given charge of five cities, and the third was declared wicked. His mina was taken from him and then given to the servant who gained ten.

This parable teaches us that:

- Good managers are rewarded.
- Bad managers and the fearful are punished.
- Bank investment is the type of investment that pays the least.

Luke 22:2-6

2 And the chief priests and the scribes sought how they might kill Him, for they feared the people.

3 Then Satan entered Judas, surnamed Iscariot, who was numbered among the twelve.

4 So he went his way and conferred with the chief priests and captains, how he might betray Him to them.

5 And they were glad, and agreed to give him money.

6 So he promised and sought opportunity to betray Him to them in the absence of the multitude.

Summary

Jesus is followed everywhere by the crowd. Driven by their desire to kill Jesus, the chief priests and the Scribes look for a favorable opportunity to do so. However, for fear of the crowd's reaction, they are afraid to do so. Satan enters Judas Iscariot, one of Jesus' disciples, and he goes to the chief priests and the chief guards to offer to hand Jesus over to them. Happy with such a proposal, they agree to pay Judah a sum of money if he delivers Jesus to them. From then on, Judah began to look for a favorable opportunity to deliver Jesus to them in the absence of the crowd.

Chapter 23
Money in the Book of John

John 2:13-16

13 Now the Passover of the Jews was at hand, and Jesus went up to Jerusalem.

14 And He found in the temple those who sold oxen and sheep and doves, and the money changers doing business.

15 When He had made a whip of cords, He drove them all out of the temple, with the sheep and the oxen, and poured out the changers' money and overturned the tables.

16 And He said to those who sold doves, "Take these things away! Do not make My Father's house a house of merchandise!"

Summary

Jesus goes up to Jerusalem for the Jewish Passover, enters the temple, and finds people selling cattle, sheep, and doves, as well as money changers sitting at tables. Faced with this observation, he makes himself a whip with ropes and then begins to chase all the sellers from the temple with the animals, overturning the money changers' tables and scattering their money throughout the temple. He told the dove sellers, "Take these things away! Do not make My Father's house a house of merchandise!"

Chapter 24
Money in the Book of Acts

Acts 4:34-37

34 Nor was there anyone among them who lacked; for all who were possessors of lands or houses sold them, and brought the proceeds of the things that were sold,

35 and laid them at the apostles' feet; and they distributed to each as anyone had need.

36 And Joses, who was also named Barnabas by the apostles (which is translated Son of Encouragement), a Levite of the country of Cyprus,

37 having land, sold it, and brought the money and laid it at the apostles' feet.

Summary

This passage describes life within the first Christian community in Jerusalem, where unity reigned among Christians who were one heart and one soul. There were no needy people among them because they shared everything they had and no one claimed that their possessions belonged to them. They took care of everyone's needs. In this context, a Levite from Cyprus named Barnabas sells a field he owns and brings the money to the apostles to distribute to believers in need.

This passage reveals the unity and generosity that existed in the early Church. Christians supported each other and prioritized community well-being.

Acts 7: 15-16

15 So Jacob went down to Egypt; and he died, he and our fathers.

16 And they were carried back to Shechem and laid in the tomb that Abraham bought for a sum of money from the sons of Hamor, the father of Shechem.

Summary

This passage explains how, to escape famine, Joseph had his father, Jacob, and his entire family, numbering seventy-five people, escorted to Egypt. Jacob would stay there until his death, when Joseph would organize a funeral for him worthy of a high dignitary. The remains of the patriarchs who died in Egypt were transported to Shechem and placed in the tomb which Abraham had bought, for money, from the sons of Hemor, father of Shechem. This text is part of Stephen's speech to the Sanhedrin just before his stoning, where he will review the history of the Israelites since Abraham.

Acts 8:17-24

17 Then they laid hands on them, and they received the Holy Spirit.

18 And when Simon saw that through the laying on of the apostles' hands the Holy Spirit was given, he offered them money,

19 saying, "Give me this power also, that anyone on whom I lay hands may receive the Holy Spirit."

20 But Peter said to him, "Your money perish with you, because you thought that the gift of God could be purchased with money!

21 You have neither part nor portion in this matter, for your heart is not right in the sight of God.

22 Repent therefore of this your wickedness, and pray God if perhaps the thought of your heart may be forgiven you.

23 For I see that you are poisoned by bitterness and bound by iniquity."

24 Then Simon answered and said, "Pray to the Lord for me, that none of the things which you have spoken may come upon me."

Summary

In this passage, Peter and John lay hands on the new believers in Samaria, who instantly received the Holy Spirit. Simon, a popular magician who had recently converted, is amazed by the manifestation of God's power and wants to appropriate this power at all costs. He offers money to Peter and John in order to purchase the ability to communicate the gift of the Holy Spirit through the laying on of hands. Peter reprimands him severely, telling him that his heart is not right and that his money perishes with him for thinking of acquiring the gift of God for money. Then he urges Simon to repent and pray for forgiveness, recognizing the seriousness of his actions and the need for true repentance.

Acts 24:17-27

17 "Now after many years I came to bring alms and offerings to my nation,

18 in the midst of which some Jews from Asia found me purified in the temple, neither with a mob nor with tumult.

19 They ought to have been here before you to object if they had anything against me.

20 Or else let those who are here themselves say [f]if they found any wrongdoing in me while I stood before the council,

21 unless it is for this one statement which I cried out, standing among them, 'Concerning the resurrection of the dead I am being judged by you this day.' "

22 But when Felix heard these things, having more accurate knowledge of the Way, he adjourned the proceedings and said, "When Lysias the commander comes down, I will make a decision on your case."

23 So he commanded the centurion to keep Paul and to let him have liberty, and told him not to forbid any of his friends to provide for or visit him.

24 And after some days, when Felix came with his wife Drusilla, who was Jewish, he sent for Paul and heard him concerning the faith in Christ.

25 Now as he reasoned about righteousness, self-control, and the judgment to come, Felix was afraid and answered, "Go away for now; when I have a convenient time I will call for you."

26 Meanwhile he also hoped that money would be given him by Paul, [g]that he might release him. Therefore he sent for him more often and conversed with him.

27 But after two years Porcius Festus succeeded Felix; and Felix, wanting to do the Jews a favor, left Paul bound.

Summary

Arriving in Caesarea, Paul is taken before Governor Felix to be interviewed. During his plea, Paul explains that he was accused without any reason when he had come to Jerusalem after a long absence to give alms and to present offerings. He specifies that he was accused of tumult even though he was found purified in the temple, without crowds or tumult. Felix, who is well-versed in the teachings of Christianity, adjourns the hearing and keeps Paul in detention, granting him some liberties. He purposely drags out the trial and frequently speaks with him in private in the hope of being offered a bribe from Paul in exchange for his release. To please the Jewish leaders and maintain political favor, Governor Felix leaves the Apostle Paul in prison for two years until his term as governor comes to an end.

Chapter 25
Money in the Book of 1 Timothy

1 Timothy 6:1-10

1 Let as many bondservants as are under the yoke count their own masters worthy of all honor, so that the name of God and His doctrine may not be blasphemed.

2 And those who have believing masters, let them not despise them because they are brethren, but rather serve them because those who are benefited are believers and beloved. Teach and exhort these things.

3 If anyone teaches otherwise and does not consent to wholesome words, even the words of our Lord Jesus Christ, and to the doctrine which accords with godliness,

4 he is proud, knowing nothing, but is obsessed with disputes and arguments over words, from which come envy, strife, reviling, evil suspicions,

5 useless wranglings of men of corrupt minds and destitute of the truth, who suppose that godliness is a means of gain. From such withdraw yourself.

6 Now godliness with contentment is great gain.

7 For we brought nothing into this world, and it is certain we can carry nothing out.

8 And having food and clothing, with these we shall be content.

9 But those who desire to be rich fall into temptation and a snare, and into many foolish and harmful lusts which drown men in destruction and perdition.

10 For the love of money is a root of all kinds of evil, for which some have strayed from the faith in their greediness, and pierced themselves through with many sorrows.

Summary

In this text, Paul begins by asking Christian servants to respect their unbelieving masters so that the name of God and his doctrine are not blasphemed. Likewise, he invites servants who have believing masters not to disrespect them but to serve them with even more ardor because they are brothers in the faith. He recommends that Timothy continue to teach and exhort in this sense. Paul declares that anyone who teaches contrary to the teaching he gives concerning the relationships between servants and masters rejects the very words of the Lord Jesus Christ and the doctrine which is according to godliness. Such teachers can be called proud and ignorant. They have corrupt minds, love arguments, and are deprived of the truth. They believe that those who practice godliness do so only to attract financial gain. Paul urges Timothy to stay away from these men. Because if godliness accompanied by contentment can bring wealth, wealth is not the ultimate goal. Religious leaders, for whom the motivation is money, fall into temptation and many senseless and harmful lusts, which lead them to their downfall like so many other men. The love of money is the basis of all that is evil; leaders who allow themselves to be caught in this trap have strayed from the faith and are prey to great torment.

This passage highlights the importance of leaders maintaining a Christ-centered life and not being drawn into ministry by financial motives. He warns of the dangers associated with such motives for these leaders.

Part 2 – Moneychangers in the Bible

Chapter 26
Moneychangers in the Book of Matthew

Matthew 21:10-13

10 And when he was come into Jerusalem, all the city was moved, saying, Who is this?

11 And the multitude said, This is Jesus the prophet of Nazareth of Galilee.

12 And Jesus went into the temple of God, and cast out all them that sold and bought in the temple, and overthrew the tables of the moneychangers, and the seats of them that sold doves,

13 And said unto them, It is written, My house shall be called the house of prayer; but ye have made it a den of thieves.

Summary

Following his triumphal entry into Jerusalem, Jesus goes to the Temple. Once there, he began to chase away everyone who was trading in the temple. He overturns the tables of those who exchanged the money and furniture of the sellers of doves. He reminds them that God had declared that His house (the Temple) will be called a house of prayer. However, they transformed it into a den of thieves.

Chapter 27
Moneychangers in the Book of Mark

Mark 11:11-19

11 And Jesus went into Jerusalem and into the temple. So when He had looked around at all things, as the hour was already late, He went out to Bethany with the twelve.

12 Now the next day, when they had come out from Bethany, He was hungry.

13 And seeing from afar a fig tree having leaves, He went to see if perhaps He would find something on it. When He came to it, He found nothing but leaves, for it was not the season for figs.

14 In response Jesus said to it, "Let no one eat fruit from you ever again."

And His disciples heard it.

15 So they came to Jerusalem. Then Jesus went into the temple and began to drive out those who bought and sold in the temple, and overturned the tables of the money changers and the seats of those who sold doves.

16 And He would not allow anyone to carry wares through the temple.

17 Then He taught, saying to them, "Is it not written, 'My house shall be called a house of prayer for all nations'? But you have made it a 'den of thieves.'"

18 And the scribes and chief priests heard it and sought how they might destroy Him; for they feared Him, because all the people were astonished at His teaching.

19 When evening had come, He went out of the city.

Summary

Arriving in Jerusalem, Jesus goes directly to visit the temple. There, he makes his observations, and, as it is already late, he leaves for Bethany with his disciples to spend the night. The next day, after leaving Bethany to go back to the temple in Jerusalem, Jesus was hungry. Having seen a fig tree from afar, he went there in the hope of finding fruit. Not having found any, he cursed the fig tree. Arriving at the temple, he begins to chase away all those who bought and sold there. He overturned the tables of those who traded currencies and the seats of those who sold doves without letting anyone take anything from the temple. Then he began to teach the people, saying, "Is it not written, My house shall be called a house of prayer for all nations? But you have made it a den of thieves." When the chief priests and the scribes heard it, they sought ways to put him to death. They fear him because of his influence on the crowd, which is attentive to his teaching. Jesus leaves the city with his disciples during the night.

It is important to note that Jesus drives out those who were dealing in currency and overturns their tables without allowing them to take the money.

Part 3 – Prosperity in the Bible

Chapter 28
Prosperity in the Book of Deuteronomy

Deuteronomy 23:3-6

3 "An Ammonite or Moabite shall not enter the assembly of the Lord; even to the tenth generation none of his descendants shall enter the assembly of the Lord forever,

4 because they did not meet you with bread and water on the road when you came out of Egypt, and because they hired against you Balaam the son of Beor from Pethor of Mesopotamia, to curse you.

5 Nevertheless the Lord your God would not listen to Balaam, but the Lord your God turned the curse into a blessing for you, because the Lord your God loves you.

6 You shall not seek their peace nor their prosperity all your days forever.

Summary

In this passage, Moses informs the Israelites that the Ammonites and Moabites, as well as their descendants, even to the tenth generation, should not enter the assembly of God. Then he explains that this exclusion is due to the fact that the Ammonites and Moabites did not provide assistance to the Israelites during their journey out of Egypt. Rather, they hired Balaam to curse the children of Israel. However, God changed the curse into a blessing for them. Moses commands the Israelites not to worry about the prosperity or well-being of the Ammonites and Moabites in perpetuity.

Chapter 29
Prosperity in the Book of Samuel

1 Samuel 25:4-8

4 When David heard in the wilderness that Nabal was shearing his sheep,

5 David sent ten young men; and David said to the young men, "Go up to Carmel, go to Nabal, and greet him in my name.

6 And thus you shall say to him who lives in prosperity: 'Peace be to you, peace to your house, and peace to all that you have!

7 Now I have heard that you have shearers. Your shepherds were with us, and we did not hurt them, nor was there anything missing from them all the while they were in Carmel.

8 Ask your young men, and they will tell you. Therefore let my young men find favor in your eyes, for we come on a feast day. Please give whatever comes to your hand to your servants and to your son David.' "

Summary

Nabal, a super-rich man from Maon, goes to Carmel, accompanied by his wife Abigail, to shear his sheep. David sends ten young men to greet him in his name saying these words: "To him who lives in prosperity, peace to you, peace to your house, and peace to all that you have!" Then he reminds him that they protected his flock and his shepherds during their stay in Carmel and that nothing was stolen, which his servants can attest. David asks him to send him some provisions—only what he finds on hand.

Chapter 30
Prosperity in the Book of 1 Kings

1 Kings 10:1-13

1 Now when the queen of Sheba heard of the fame of Solomon concerning the name of the Lord, she came to test him with hard questions.

2 She came to Jerusalem with a very great retinue, with camels that bore spices, very much gold, and precious stones; and when she came to Solomon, she spoke with him about all that was in her heart.

3 So Solomon answered all her questions; there was nothing so difficult for the king that he could not explain it to her.

4 And when the queen of Sheba had seen all the wisdom of Solomon, the house that he had built,

5 the food on his table, the seating of his servants, the service of his waiters and their apparel, his cupbearers, and his entryway by which he went up to the house of the Lord, there was no more spirit in her.

6 Then she said to the king: "It was a true report which I heard in my own land about your words and your wisdom.

7 However I did not believe the words until I came and saw with my own eyes; and indeed the half was not told me. Your wisdom and prosperity exceed the fame of which I heard.

8 Happy are your men and happy are these your servants, who stand continually before you and hear your wisdom!

9 Blessed be the Lord your God, who delighted in you, setting you on the throne of Israel! Because the Lord has loved Israel forever, therefore He made you king, to do justice and righteousness."

10 Then she gave the king one hundred and twenty talents of gold, spices in great quantity, and precious stones. There never again came such abundance of spices as the queen of Sheba gave to King Solomon.

11 Also, the ships of Hiram, which brought gold from Ophir, brought great quantities of almug wood and precious stones from Ophir.

12 And the king made steps of the almug wood for the house of the Lord and for the king's house, also harps and stringed instruments for singers. There never again came such almug wood, nor has the like been seen to this day.

13 Now King Solomon gave the queen of Sheba all she desired, whatever she asked, besides what Solomon had given her according to the royal generosity. So she turned and went to her own country, she and her servants.

Summary

Having heard of Solomon's wisdom and wealth, the Queen of Sheba makes an official visit to Jerusalem to see for herself. She arrives there with a strong escort and camels carrying spices, gold, and precious stones in large quantities. During her meeting with King Solomon, the Queen of Sheba questions him on all kinds of subjects and presents him with different types of enigmas. In return, Solomon answers all her questions and solves all her enigmas. During her stay, the queen took the time to visit, observe, and appreciate the quality of the meals served, the dress and posture of Solomon's servants, their houses, the protocol, the beauty of the royal palace, and even the sacrifices offered by King Solomon. She marvels at the wisdom and wealth of Solomon, the prosperity of his kingdom, his officials, and the splendor of his palace. Overwhelmed, the Queen of Sheba praised Solomon, recognizing that what she had heard of Solomon's wisdom and wealth was no match for what she had seen and experienced personally. She claims that they widely exceed everything that was said. The queen praises the Lord and gives as a gift to King Solomon 120 talents of gold, precious stones, a large quantity of sandalwood, and spices in quantities never equaled in Israel. For his part, King Solomon grants her everything she desires, everything she asks for in addition to the royal gifts.

Chapter 31
Prosperity in the Book of Job

Job 15:20-22

20 The wicked man writhes with pain all his days, And the number of years is hidden from the oppressor.

21 Dreadful sounds are in his ears; In prosperity the destroyer comes upon him.

22 He does not believe that he will return from darkness, For a sword is waiting for him.

Summary

In this passage, we find one of Job's friends, Eliphaz, giving him a speech about the wicked. It presents the villain as someone who lives in torment and anguish throughout his life. Constantly troubled and agitated, he always hears terrifying sounds. Even in prosperity, where he should have been safe, the destroyer terrorizes him and strikes him. Knowing that a sword awaits him around the corner, he lives in constant fear. This passage highlights Eliphaz's belief that Job's suffering was likely due to the inevitable consequences of a bad life and his own wrongdoings.

Job 36:5-12

5 "Behold, God is mighty, but despises no one; He is mighty in strength of understanding.

6 He does not preserve the life of the wicked, But gives justice to the oppressed.

7 He does not withdraw His eyes from the righteous; But they are on the throne with kings, For He has seated them forever, And they are exalted.

8 And if they are bound in fetters, Held in the cords of affliction,

9 Then He tells them their work and their transgressions—That they have acted defiantly.

10 He also opens their ear to instruction, And commands that they turn from iniquity.

11 If they obey and serve Him, They shall spend their days in prosperity, And their years in pleasures.

12 But if they do not obey, They shall perish by the sword, And they shall die without knowledge.

Summary

This passage presents the continuity of the speech of Elihu, one of Job's friends, who affirms that God is all powerful in strength and wisdom and rejects no one. He does not let the wicked live, but He does justice to the unfortunate and preserves the righteous, whom He elevates by placing them forever on the throne with kings. When the righteous stumble and fall, God shows them their transgressions, warns them for their instruction, and exhorts them to turn from iniquity. If they obey and serve Him, they will end their days in prosperity and joy. Otherwise, they will perish by the sword.

Chapter 32
Prosperity in the Book of Psalms

Psalms 30:1-12

1 I will extol You, O Lord, for You have lifted me up, And have not let my foes rejoice over me.

2 O Lord my God, I cried out to You, And You healed me.

3 O Lord, You brought my soul up from the grave; You have kept me alive, that I should not go down to the pit.

4 Sing praise to the Lord, you saints of His, And give thanks at the remembrance of His holy name.

5 For His anger is but for a moment, His favor is for life; Weeping may endure for a night, But joy comes in the morning.

6 Now in my prosperity I said, "I shall never be moved."

7 Lord, by Your favor You have made my mountain stand strong; You hid Your face, and I was troubled.

8 I cried out to You, O Lord; And to the Lord I made supplication:

9 "What profit is there in my blood, When I go down to the pit? Will the dust praise You? Will it declare Your truth?

10 Hear, O Lord, and have mercy on me; Lord, be my helper!"

11 You have turned for me my mourning into dancing; You have put off my sackcloth and clothed me with gladness,

12 To the end that my glory may sing praise to You and not be silent. O Lord my God, I will give thanks to You forever.

Summary

This passage is a prayer of thanksgiving made by King David on the occasion of the inauguration of his house. He begins by glorifying God for exalting him and not letting his enemies rejoice over him. He recalls the occasions when he cried out to God; God healed him and preserved his soul from death. He invites the saints to praise and thank God by remembering his holiness. David mentions that God's wrath lasts only a moment, so his favor lasts a lifetime; the crying lasts a night, while the cries of joy last until the morning. In his prosperity, David declares, "I will never be shaken." By his favor the Lord has established the mountain of David, who was troubled when the Lord hid his face from him. In his anguish he pleaded with God, saying, "What profit is there in my blood, When I go down to the pit? Shall the dust praise you? Will it declare your truth? Listen, Lord, and have mercy on me; Lord, be my helper!" God transformed his lamentations into joy and exchanged his clothes of sackcloth for clothes of joy. David promises God that, until the end, his glory will sing the praises of the Lord and will not be silent and that he will thank Him forever.

Psalms 35:26-28

26 Let them be ashamed and brought to mutual confusion Who rejoice at my hurt; Let them be clothed with shame and dishonor Who exalt themselves against me.

27 Let them shout for joy and be glad, Who favor my righteous cause; And let them say continually, "Let the Lord be magnified, Who has pleasure in the prosperity of His servant."

28 And my tongue shall speak of Your righteousness And of Your praise all the day long.

Summary

In this passage, David appeals to God's justice to avenge his enemies and prevent them from rejoicing over him. He declares that those who rejoice in his disappointments and who exalt themselves against him should be confused, plunged into shame and dishonor. Conversely, let those who ally themselves with his just cause be rejoicing and joyful. Let them continually say, "May the Lord be exalted, who delights in the prosperity of his servant." In return, David promises to praise God and speak of His righteousness all the day long.

Psalms 73:1-3

1 Truly God is good to Israel, To such as are pure in heart.

2 But as for me, my feet had almost stumbled; My steps had nearly slipped.

3 For I was envious of the boastful, When I saw the prosperity of the wicked.

Summary

This passage illustrates the observation made by the psalmist Asaph on the apparent prosperity of the wicked in comparison to the righteous. By looking at the wicked, the psalmist notes that they are firm, prosper, and do not experience suffering like the rest of men while they are haughty, deny God, and speak and act wickedly without regard for morality. Faced with this picture, Asaph admits that he almost succumbed to temptation and lost his footing. But when he enters the sanctuaries of God and contemplates the end of the wicked, whom God places on slippery paths, brings to ruin, and suddenly annihilates, Asaph repents and confesses his stupidity and his lack of intelligence.

Psalms 118:25

Save now, I pray, O Lord; O Lord, I pray, send now prosperity.

Summary

This text is taken from a much larger thanksgiving hymn. It reflects complete dependence on God for both his protection and his continued blessings. The psalmist calls on God to ask for deliverance and prosperity.

Psalms 122:2-7

2 Our feet have been standing Within your gates, O Jerusalem!

3 Jerusalem is built As a city that is compact together,

4 Where the tribes go up, The tribes of the Lord, To the Testimony of Israel, To give thanks to the name of the Lord.

5 For thrones are set there for judgment, The thrones of the house of David.

6 Pray for the peace of Jerusalem: "May they prosper who love you.

7 Peace be within your walls, Prosperity within your palaces."

Summary

In these verses, the psalmist David expresses his joy at the idea of going to the house of the Lord in Jerusalem. He then praises Jerusalem, which he describes as:

- the place of meeting, testimony, and expression of thanksgiving of the tribes of Israel
- the place of installation of the thrones of God's judgment and the thrones of the house of David

The psalmist invites us to pray for the peace of Jerusalem and declares that:

- those who love the city may prosper
- peace be within its walls
- prosperity be in his palaces

Chapter 33
Prosperity in the Book of Proverbs

Proverbs 1:24-32

24 Because I have called, and ye refused; I have stretched out my hand, and no man regarded;

25 But ye have set at nought all my counsel, and would none of my reproof:

26 I also will laugh at your calamity; I will mock when your fear cometh;

27 When your fear cometh as desolation, and your destruction cometh as a whirlwind; when distress and anguish cometh upon you.

28 Then shall they call upon me, but I will not answer; they shall seek me early, but they shall not find me:

29 For that they hated knowledge, and did not choose the fear of the Lord:

30 They would none of my counsel: they despised all my reproof.

31 Therefore shall they eat of the fruit of their own way, and be filled with their own devices.

32 For the turning away of the simple shall slay them, and the prosperity of fools shall destroy them.

Summary

In this passage, Wisdom, who is personified, speaks of the consequences of ignoring her advice. She informs that since:

- his appeals were resisted
- his outstretched hand is ignored
- his advice was rejected
- and his reprimands were not appreciated

she also will laugh when they are in misfortune and mock when they are in terror and distress.

In these moments, they will seek Wisdom but will not find it. They will eat the fruit of their way and be satisfied with their own means. Wisdom ends by declaring that the resistance of the stupid will kill them and their prosperity will be their downfall.

Chapter 34
Prosperity in the Book of Ecclesiastes

Ecclesiastes 7:11-14

11 Wisdom is good with an inheritance, And profitable to those who see the sun.

12 For wisdom is a defense as money is a defense, But the excellence of knowledge is that wisdom gives life to those who have it.

13 Consider the work of God; For who can make straight what He has made crooked?

14 In the day of prosperity be joyful, But in the day of adversity consider: Surely God has appointed the one as well as the other, So that man can find out nothing that will come after him.

Summary

In this passage, Solomon teaches about the relationship between wisdom and money. He begins by mentioning that:

- wisdom goes perfectly with an inheritance.
- both wisdom and money are protections for those who possess them.

He further states that while wisdom gives life to its possessor, among the two, only money has the capacity to take it back. He ends up recommending the attitude to display in times of prosperity and adversity. If he encourages people to be joyful in times of prosperity, he invites them in adversity to consider that God created both prosperity and adversity so that man cannot discover what will come after him.

Chapter 35
Prosperity in the Book of Jeremiah

Jeremiah 22:20-22

20 "Go up to Lebanon, and cry out, And lift up your voice in Bashan; Cry from Abarim, For all your lovers are destroyed.

21 I spoke to you in your prosperity, But you said, 'I will not hear.' This has been your manner from your youth, That you did not obey My voice.

22 The wind shall eat up all your rulers, And your lovers shall go into captivity; Surely then you will be ashamed and humiliated For all your wickedness.

Summary

In this passage, which presents Jeremiah's prophecy about the house of the king of Judah, God commands Jeremiah to prophesy about the territories of Lebanon, Bashan, and Abarim. Through the mouth of Jeremiah, God informs them that their lovers are destroyed and reminds them that, in their moment of prosperity, He had called them but they had refused to listen to Him, as they have done since their youth, by disobeying His voice. Because of this, the wind will devour their leaders and their loves will all go into captivity. So, they will be humiliated and ashamed because of their wickedness.

Jeremiah 33:6-9

6 Behold, I will bring it health and healing; I will heal them and reveal to them the abundance of peace and truth.

7 And I will cause the captives of Judah and the captives of Israel to return, and will rebuild those places as at the first.

8 I will cleanse them from all their iniquity by which they have sinned against Me, and I will pardon all their iniquities by which they have sinned and by which they have transgressed against Me.

9 Then it shall be to Me a name of joy, a praise, and an honor before all nations of the earth, who shall hear all the good that I do to them; they shall fear and tremble for all the goodness and all the prosperity that I provide for it.'

Summary

This passage presents Jeremiah's prophecy on the fall and even captivity of the kingdom of Judah in Babylon and its restoration. This portion of text indeed tells us about this restoration process. God promises to:

- give healing and health, abundant peace, and fidelity to the city of Jerusalem
- bring back Judah and the children of Israel from captivity
- restore them to their past glory
- purify them of their iniquity
- forgive them their faults
- make Jerusalem a subject of joy, praise, and honor before the nations who will hear of the mercy of God toward the children of Israel

In response, they will fear and tremble at all the goodness and prosperity that God will bring to his people.

Chapter 36
Prosperity in the Book of Lamentations

Lamentations 3:16-17

16 He has also broken my teeth with gravel, And covered me with ashes.

17 You have moved my soul far from peace; I have forgotten prosperity.

Summary

This passage is describing the anguish and deep despair faced by the suffering experienced by the prophet Jeremiah, who feels humiliated and broken. He feels like God has knocked his teeth out with gravel and covered him in ashes. He feels deprived of peace to the point of forgetting what prosperity is.

Chapter 37
Prosperity in the Book of Zechariah

Zechariah 1:16-17

16 'Therefore thus says the Lord: "I am returning to Jerusalem with mercy; My house shall be built in it," says the Lord of hosts, "And a surveyor's line shall be stretched out over Jerusalem." '

17 "Again proclaim, saying, 'Thus says the Lord of hosts: "My cities shall again spread out through prosperity; The Lord will again comfort Zion, And will again choose Jerusalem." ' "

Summary

In this passage, God communicates to Zechariah the prophecy about the restoration of the city of Jerusalem. He promises that he will return to the city with mercy and rebuild it and that a measuring line will be stretched over Jerusalem. Additionally, God asks Zechariah to proclaim that his cities will once again expand through prosperity and that the Lord will once again comfort Zion and choose Jerusalem.

Zechariah 7:4-7

4 Then came the word of the Lord of hosts unto me, saying,

5 Speak unto all the people of the land, and to the priests, saying, When ye fasted and mourned in the fifth and seventh month, even those seventy years, did ye at all fast unto me, even to me?

6 And when ye did eat, and when ye did drink, did not ye eat for yourselves, and drink for yourselves?

7 Should ye not hear the words which the Lord hath cried by the former prophets, when Jerusalem was inhabited and in prosperity, and the cities thereof round about her, when men inhabited the south and the plain?

Summary

In this text, God addresses the following questions to the people and the priests through the prophet Zechariah:

1- When you fasted and mourned in the fifth and seventh months during these seventy years, did you really fast for Me?

2- When you eat and drink, aren't you doing it for yourself?

3- Should you not have obeyed the words that the Lord proclaimed through the ancient prophets, when Jerusalem and the surrounding cities were inhabited and in prosperity?

Part 4 – Wealth in the Bible

Chapter 38
Wealth in the Book of Genesis

Genesis 34:27-29

27 The sons of Jacob came upon the slain, and plundered the city, because their sister had been defiled.

28 They took their sheep, their oxen, and their donkeys, what was in the city and what was in the field,

29 and all their wealth. All their little ones and their wives they took captive; and they plundered even all that was in the houses.

Summary

To wash away the shame caused by the rape of their sister Dinah by Shechem, Simeon and Levi attack the men of the city while they are still in pain following their circumcision. They kill them all, including Hamor, Shechem's father. Then they take Dinah back and plunder the city, taking as booty the women and children, all the wealth, all the livestock, and everything found in the houses and in the fields.

Chapter 39
Wealth in the Book of Deuteronomy

Deuteronomy 8:11-20

11 "Beware that you do not forget the Lord your God by not keeping His commandments, His judgments, and His statutes which I command you today,

12 lest—when you have eaten and are full, and have built beautiful houses and dwell in them;

13 and when your herds and your flocks multiply, and your silver and your gold are multiplied, and all that you have is multiplied;

14 when your heart is lifted up, and you forget the Lord your God who brought you out of the land of Egypt, from the house of bondage;

15 who led you through that great and terrible wilderness, in which were fiery serpents and scorpions and thirsty land where there was no water; who brought water for you out of the flinty rock;

16 who fed you in the wilderness with manna, which your fathers did not know, that He might humble you and that He might test you, to do you good in the end—

17 then you say in your heart, 'My power and the might of my hand have gained me this wealth.'

18 "And you shall remember the Lord your God, for it is He who gives you power to get wealth, that He may establish His covenant which He swore to your fathers, as it is this day.

19 Then it shall be, if you by any means forget the Lord your God, and follow other gods, and serve them and worship them, I testify against you this day that you shall surely perish.

20 As the nations which the Lord destroys before you, so you shall perish, because you would not be obedient to the voice of the Lord your God.

Summary

In this passage, Moses warns the Israelites to remember their God, who brought them out of Egypt, protected them, and led them through the wilderness. He asks them to:

- Remember to keep His commandments, decrees, and laws when they are in the Promised Land, eating and being satisfied, building beautiful houses, and seeing their livestock, silver, and gold multiply

- Beware that their hearts do not become arrogant and forget that it was the Lord who brought them out of Egypt and led them through the wilderness.

Moses reminds them of the difficulties they encountered in the wilderness, such as snakes, scorpions, and the lack of water and food, as well as the miracles that God performed to bring them deliverance at that time, even making water come out of a rock to give them water and manna fall from heaven to feed them. Moses also warns them to say in their hearts that their wealth is the fruit of their power and might.

Finally, Moses warns them that if they forget the LORD and follow other gods, worshiping them and bowing down to them, they will surely be destroyed like the nations whom God drove out before them. Disobedience will result in their destruction for not obeying the LORD their God.

Chapter 40
Wealth in the Book of Ruth

Ruth 2:1

1 There was a relative of Naomi's husband, a man of great wealth, of the family of Elimelech. His name was Boaz.

Summary

This verse presents Boaz, a relative of Naomi's deceased husband, as a powerful man, possessing a very large fortune and coming from the family of Elimelech. He will marry by right of redemption Ruth, the Moabitess, daughter-in-law of Naomi, who will bear him Obed, who will later become the father of Jesse, father of David.

Chapter 41
Wealth in the Book of 1 Samuel

1 Samuel 2:27-32

27 And there came a man of God unto Eli, and said unto him, Thus saith the Lord, Did I plainly appear unto the house of thy father, when they were in Egypt in Pharaoh's house?

28 And did I choose him out of all the tribes of Israel to be my priest, to offer upon mine altar, to burn incense, to wear an ephod before me? and did I give unto the house of thy father all the offerings made by fire of the children of Israel?

29 Wherefore kick ye at my sacrifice and at mine offering, which I have commanded in my habitation; and honourest thy sons above me, to make yourselves fat with the chiefest of all the offerings of Israel my people?

30 Wherefore the Lord God of Israel saith, I said indeed that thy house, and the house of thy father, should walk before me for ever: but now the Lord saith, Be it far from me; for them that honour me I will honour, and they that despise me shall be lightly esteemed.

31 Behold, the days come, that I will cut off thine arm, and the arm of thy father's house, that there shall not be an old man in thine house.

32 And thou shalt see an enemy in my habitation, in all the wealth which God shall give Israel: and there shall not be an old man in thine house for ever.

Summary

In this passage, a man of God comes to deliver a message to the priest Eli. He begins by communicating these three questions from the Lord:

1- Did I not fully reveal myself to your father's house, when they were in Egypt in Pharaoh's house?

2- Why do you trample underfoot my sacrifices and my offerings, which I commanded to be made in my dwelling?

3- Why is it that you honor your sons more than me, to make yourselves fat with the first fruits of all the offerings of Israel, my people?

God reminds Eli that He chose his father's house from all the tribes of Israel to be at his service in the priesthood to go up to his altar, to burn incense, and to wear the ephod before Him, and that he gave to his father's house all the offerings consumed by fire and offered by the children of Israel. Because of the sinful actions of Eli's sons and Eli's failure to rebuke them, God tells him that although He had originally promised that his house and his father's house would serve before Him forever, that promise is now revoked because Eli's family has not honored Him and He will cut off his arm and the arm of his father's house so that there will no longer be an old man in his house. Furthermore, God informs him that he will see an enemy in the Temple, in the midst of all the wealth He will give to Israel, and that all those of his house will die in the flower of their youth.

Chapter 42
Wealth in the Book of 2 Kings

2 Kings 15:19-20

19 Pul king of Assyria came against the land; and Menahem gave Pul a thousand talents of silver, that his hand might be with him to strengthen the kingdom under his control.

20 And Menahem exacted the money from Israel, from all the very wealthy, from each man fifty shekels of silver, to give to the king of Assyria. So the king of Assyria turned back, and did not stay there in the land.

Summary

Pul, king of Assyria, came with his army to besiege Israel. To save the country, Menahem, king of Israel, paid a tribute of a thousand talents of silver to the king of Assyria in order to make an alliance with him to strengthen his kingdom. To raise this sum, Menahem exacted money from all those who had wealth in Israel; he taxed each of them to pay fifty shekels of silver on behalf of the king of Assyria. After receiving this money, the king of Assyria returned to his country with his army.

Chapter 43
Wealth in the Book of 2 Chronicles

2 Chronicles 1:7-12

7 On that night God appeared to Solomon, and said to him, "Ask! What shall I give you?"

8 And Solomon said to God: "You have shown great mercy to David my father, and have made me king in his place.

9 Now, O Lord God, let Your promise to David my father be established, for You have made me king over a people like the dust of the earth in multitude.

10 Now give me wisdom and knowledge, that I may go out and come in before this people; for who can judge this great people of Yours?"

11 Then God said to Solomon: "Because this was in your heart, and you have not asked riches or wealth or honor or the life of your enemies, nor have you asked long life—but have asked wisdom and knowledge for yourself, that you may judge My people over whom I have made you king—

12 wisdom and knowledge are granted to you; and I will give you riches and wealth and honor, such as none of the kings have had who were before you, nor shall any after you have the like."

Summary

This passage describes God's famous encounter with Solomon. Following the temple dedication festivities, God comes to Solomon in a dream and asks Solomon what he wants Him to give him. After reviewing God's expression of mercy to his father David and recalling that his accession to the throne is the fulfillment of God's promise to his father, Solomon asks God to grant him wisdom and understanding so that he will know how to lead the people well. In response, God said to him, "Because this is what is in your heart, and you do not ask for riches or wealth or honor or the death of your enemies or even long life, but you ask for yourself wisdom and understanding, so that you may judge my people over whom I have made you king, wisdom and understanding are granted to you." He also said to Solomon, "I will give you riches, wealth, and honor, such as no king before you has had, nor will any king after you have had." These verses emphasize Solomon's priority of acquiring wisdom and knowledge over wealth and power. This particularly pleases God, who responds by granting him wealth, fortune, and honor in addition to wisdom and knowledge, making him the wisest and wealthiest king who has ever lived.

Chapter 44
Wealth in the Book of Ezra

Ezra 9:10-12 (KJV)

10 And now, O our God, what shall we say after this? for we have forsaken thy commandments,

11 Which thou hast commanded by thy servants the prophets, saying, The land, unto which ye go to possess it, is an unclean land with the filthiness of the people of the lands, with their abominations, which have filled it from one end to another with their uncleanness.

12 Now therefore give not your daughters unto their sons, neither take their daughters unto your sons, nor seek their peace or their wealth for ever: that ye may be strong, and eat the good of the land, and leave it for an inheritance to your children for ever.

Summary

This passage is taken from Ezra's prayer of lamentation over the disobedience of the people of Israel.

The leaders come to inform Ezra that the people, the priests and the Levites have not separated themselves from the Canaanites, the Hittites, the Perizzites, the Jebusites, the Ammonites, the Moabites, the Egyptians, and the Amorites who surround the territory of Israel, that they imitate their abominations and bind themselves to them by marriage. Ezra, dismayed by the actions of the children of Israel, tears his clothes and pulls out his hair and beard. At the time of the evening sacrifice, he addresses a prayer to God in which he expresses his confusion and shame. Indeed, he emphasizes that despite the number and gravity of the sins of the children of Israel that reach to the heavens, God did not exterminate them all and still showed them mercy by leaving a few survivors. When they were deported into captivity, He did not leave them in servitude. They abandoned God's commandments that told them not to marry or marry their daughters to the sons of these nations or to marry their sons to the daughters of these nations and never to worry about their wealth or their peace. Despite everything, God continued to show mercy to the people of Israel.

Chapter 45
Wealth in the Book of Esther

Esther 10:3

3 For Mordecai the Jew was next unto king Ahasuerus, and great among the Jews, and accepted of the multitude of his brethren, seeking the wealth of his people, and speaking peace to all his seed.

Summary

This text, which ends the book of Esther, presents to us in a few words the character of Mordecai. He is Jewish and the first most important person, after King Ahasuerus, in the kingdom of Babylon. He is respected and loved among the Jews and by the multitude of his brothers. He seeks the prosperity of his people and speaks for the happiness of his whole race.

Chapter 46
Wealth in the Book of Job

Job 21:13

13 They spend their days in wealth, and in a moment go down to the grave.

Summary

This passage is taken from Job's plea for the wicked. He questions their reason for being and wonders why they are seen to grow old and increase in strength. He notes that:

- their posterity is established before their eyes.
- their houses are protected from fear.
- the rod of God does not strike them.
- their businesses prosper, are established, and grow.
- their children are safe.
- they are joyful and celebrate.
- they spend their days in wealth and suddenly die.

Job 31:24-28

24 "If I have made gold my hope, Or said to fine gold, 'You are my confidence';

25 If I have rejoiced because my wealth was great, And because my hand had gained much;

26 If I have observed the sun when it shines, Or the moon moving in brightness,

27 So that my heart has been secretly enticed, And my mouth has kissed my hand;

28 This also would be an iniquity deserving of judgment, For I would have denied God who is above.

Summary

This passage is an excerpt from Job's long speech in defense of his integrity before his three friends. He states that he would have deserved God's judgment if he:

- had placed his hope in gold
- had said to fine gold, "You are my confidence"
- had rejoiced in the abundance of his wealth or the goods he had acquired with his hands
- had worshiped the sun and the moon

If he had done any of these things, it would be considered a denial of God.

For Job, who sees his suffering as a form of judgment from God, God's judgment would be understandable if he had devoted a cult of worship to his great wealth or made celestial bodies, such as the sun or the moon, objects of worship. This text highlights Job's commitment to identify and distance himself from greed and idolatry and to remain faithful to God.

Chapter 47
Wealth in the Book of Psalms

Psalms 44:9-12

9 But You have cast us off and put us to shame, And You do not go out with our armies.

10 You make us turn back from the enemy, And those who hate us have taken spoil for themselves.

11 You have given us up like sheep intended for food, And have scattered us among the nations.

12 You sell Your people for next to nothing, And are not enriched by selling them.

Summary

This song of the Sons of Korah tells of the present situation of the people of Israel and recalls the past glory.

The Sons of Korah describe the situation of the Jews, who are rejected by God and plunged into shame; the army is abandoned by God on the battlefields. As a result, they retreat before their enemies and are plundered; they are delivered like sheep and scattered among the nations; they are devalued and sold for almost nothing, to the point that the profit from their sale does not affect God's wealth in any way.

Psalms 49:1-10

1 Hear this, all peoples; Give ear, all inhabitants of the world,

2 Both low and high, Rich and poor together.

3 My mouth shall speak wisdom, And the meditation of my heart shall give understanding.

4 I will incline my ear to a proverb; I will disclose my dark saying on the harp.

5 Why should I fear in the days of evil, When the iniquity at my heels surrounds me?

6 Those who trust in their wealth And boast in the multitude of their riches,

7 None of them can by any means redeem his brother, Nor give to God a ransom for him—

8 For the redemption of their souls is costly, And it shall cease forever—

9 That he should continue to live eternally, And not see the Pit.

10 For he sees wise men die; Likewise the fool and the senseless person perish, And leave their wealth to others.

Summary

Psalm 49 is a song written by the Sons of Korah for all the inhabitants of the world, both low and high, rich and poor. The Sons of Korah invite them to receive the wisdom that comes from their mouths and the meditation that comes from their hearts. They ask why they should be afraid in evil days, when iniquity stalks them until it surrounds them. They affirm that, of those who trust in their wealth and boast in the multitude of their possessions, no one can in any way redeem his brother or give God a ransom for his life so that he continues to live forever and does not see the pit. For he sees the wise men die, just as the foolish and senseless perish and leave their wealth to others. This text conveys the message that eternal life is priceless, that wealth cannot save a person from death, and that everyone, regardless of wealth or social status, will eventually face the same fate.

Psalms 112:1-3

1 Blessed is the man who fears the Lord, Who delights greatly in His commandments.

2 His descendants will be mighty on earth; The generation of the upright will be blessed.

3 Wealth and riches will be in his house, And his righteousness endures forever.

Summary

In this text, the psalmist declares that the man who fears the Lord and delights in his precepts is blessed. Subsistence and riches will be in his house, and his righteousness will endure forever. He will raise up a generation of upright men who will be blessed, and their descendants will be mighty on earth.

Chapter 48
Wealth in the Book of Proverbs

Proverbs 5:7-14

7 Therefore hear me now, my children, And do not depart from the words of my mouth.

8 Remove your way far from her, And do not go near the door of her house,

9 Lest you give your honor to others, And your years to the cruel one;

10 Lest aliens be filled with your wealth, And your labors go to the house of a foreigner;

11 And you mourn at last, When your flesh and your body are consumed,

12 And say: "How I have hated instruction, And my heart despised correction!

13 I have not obeyed the voice of my teachers, Nor inclined my ear to those who instructed me!

14 I was on the verge of total ruin, In the midst of the assembly and congregation."

Summary

This text is a warning from Solomon to his sons against the foreign woman. He recommends that they not deviate from his teachings but instead distance themselves from everything that leads back to the foreign woman and her house. This is to prevent that:

- their honor goes to others
- their years go to a cruel man
- their wealth is transferred to foreigners to satisfy themselves
- the fruits of their labor go to benefit the house of a foreigner
- they lament at the end of their life and say: "How I have hated instruction, and my heart has despised reproof"

The word "foreigner or stranger" in the phrase "foreign or strange woman" comes from the Hebrew "רוז" (Zûr) which can be expressed as "profane in moral principles" in the context of the passage.

Proverbs 10:13-15

13 Wisdom is found on the lips of him who has understanding, But a rod is for the back of him who is devoid of understanding.

14 Wise people store up knowledge, But the mouth of the foolish is near destruction.

15 The rich man's wealth is his strong city; The destruction of the poor is their poverty.

Summary

This portion of the Scripture is taken from the wisdom of Solomon, and answers two essential questions:

1- What does wealth represent for the rich?

2- What is the greatest enemy of the poor?

As if to prepare us to receive his teaching, Solomon informs us that wisdom is found in the mouths of those who understand. For those who refuse to understand, a rod is available to punish them. Faced with new knowledge, wise people store it up, while the stupid refuse it and argue. This attitude can lead them to their downfall.

Then Solomon gives us the answers to the previous questions:

1- wealth constitutes for the rich his fortified city or his defense system.
2- While the greatest enemy of the poor, and who seeks to destroy him, is his poverty.

Proverbs 13:11

11 Wealth gained by dishonesty will be diminished, But he who gathers by labor will increase.

Summary

In this passage, Solomon teaches about the acquisition of wealth. He states that those who earn their wealth dishonestly or in haste will not be able to keep it but will lose it little by little. Conversely, those who patiently build their wealth through work will keep it and increase it.

Proverbs 13:22

22 A good man leaves an inheritance to his children's children, But the wealth of the sinner is stored up for the righteous.

Summary

In this passage Solomon highlights a notable difference between a good man and a sinner that can easily be used to compare the righteous and the wicked. He teaches us that the good man, who can be compared by the righteous:

- plans for the long term
- builds wealth for his posterity
- thinks of future generations
- has descendants
- has a long life

Conversely, the sinner, who can be compared to the wicked:

- has a short life

- does not think of future generations
- has no descendants
- does not plan for the long term
- builds wealth for the righteous

In summary, a righteous life has excellent advantages in the long term.

Proverbs 18:10-11

10 The name of the Lord is a strong tower; The righteous run to it and are safe.

11 The rich man's wealth is his strong city, And like a high wall in his own esteem.

Summary

In this text, Solomon contrasts the sources of security for both the righteous and the rich. The name of the Lord is a strong tower for the righteous, who takes refuge in it and finds himself safe. For the rich man, on his side, it is his wealth that constitutes a strong city for him. It is in his wealth that he places his trust and it is there that he feels safe. If wealth provides a certain security, it is better to place one's trust in the Lord, who is unshakable and who is the source of all security.

Proverbs 19:4

4 Wealth makes many friends, But the poor is separated from his friend.

Summary

Solomon presents in this passage the social impact of wealth and poverty. If wealth acts like a magnet and attracts people, poverty, on the contrary, repels them. Wealth gives many friends to the rich, while poverty separates the poor from his friends. So, the poorer one is, the fewer friends one has.

Chapter 49
Wealth in the Book of Ecclesiastes

Ecclesiastes 5:18-20

18 Here is what I have seen: It is good and fitting for one to eat and drink, and to enjoy the good of all his labor in which he toils under the sun all the days of his life which God gives him; for it is his heritage.

19 As for every man to whom God has given riches and wealth, and given him power to eat of it, to receive his heritage and rejoice in his labor—this is the gift of God.

20 For he will not dwell unduly on the days of his life, because God keeps him busy with the joy of his heart.

Summary

In this text, Solomon teaches us that it is good, even pleasant, for a person to take time to eat, drink, enjoy, and profit from all the work he does under the sun during the days that God has given him to live on the earth. It is even considered a reward from God. He also teaches us that the wealth and goods accumulated by a person come from God, as does the ability to use and enjoy these riches and to rejoice in the midst of his work. All of this is to be seen as a gift from God. Finally, Solomon tells us that such a person will not dwell unduly on the days of his life because God keeps him occupied with the joy of his heart.

This passage suggests that true fulfillment comes from appreciating and enjoying the wealth and goods that we receive from God daily throughout our entire lives.

Ecclesiastes 6:1-2

1 There is an evil which I have seen under the sun, and it is common among men:

2 A man to whom God has given riches and wealth and honor, so that he lacks nothing for himself of all he desires; yet God does not give him power to eat of it, but a foreigner consumes it. This is vanity, and it is an evil affliction.

Summary

Solomon presents to us in this text an evil that he has seen frequently under the sun. It concerns people to whom God has given goods, riches, and honor, who have everything they desire and lack nothing. However, God has not granted them the capacity to enjoy these blessings. On the other hand, God has granted a foreigner the privilege of making use of these goods and riches. Solomon mentions that this is a vanity and a very serious illness.

Chapter 50
Wealth in the Book of Zechariah

Zechariah 14:12-15

12 And this shall be the plague with which the Lord will strike all the people who fought against Jerusalem: Their flesh shall dissolve while they stand on their feet, Their eyes shall dissolve in their sockets, And their tongues shall dissolve in their mouths.

13 It shall come to pass in that day That a great panic from the Lord will be among them. Everyone will seize the hand of his neighbor, And raise his hand against his neighbor's hand;

14 Judah also will fight at Jerusalem. And the wealth of all the surrounding nations Shall be gathered together: Gold, silver, and apparel in great abundance.

15 Such also shall be the plague On the horse and the mule, On the camel and the donkey, And on all the cattle that will be in those camps. So shall this plague be.

Summary

In this prophetic passage, Zechariah presents to us, on the day of the Lord, the vengeance that God reserves against all the nations that will have fought against Jerusalem:

- Their flesh will rot while they are on their feet.
- Their eyes will rot in their sockets.
- Their tongue will rot in their mouth.
- The Lord will produce a great disturbance among them.

- One will take hold of another's hand, and they will lift up their hand one on another.
- Judah will also fight in Jerusalem.
- The wealth of all the nations around, The gold, the silver, and the very great number of garments will be gathered.
- The plague will strike the horses, The mules, the camels, the donkeys, and all the beasts that will be in these camps.
- All those who remain of all the nations that came against Jerusalem will go up from year to year to worship the Lord of hosts and to celebrate the feast of tabernacles.

Chapter 51
Wealth in the Book of Acts

Acts 19:23-27

23 And about that time there arose a great commotion about the Way.

24 For a certain man named Demetrius, a silversmith, who made silver shrines of Diana, brought no small profit to the craftsmen.

25 He called them together with the workers of similar occupation, and said: "Men, you know that we have our prosperity (wealth) by this trade.

26 Moreover you see and hear that not only at Ephesus, but throughout almost all Asia, this Paul has persuaded and turned away many people, saying that they are not gods which are made with hands.

27 So not only is this trade of ours in danger of falling into disrepute, but also the temple of the great goddess Diana may be despised and her magnificence destroyed, whom all Asia and the world worship."

Summary

This portion of Scripture introduces us to the uprising in Ephesus caused by Demetrius because of the impact of Paul's ministry on the local economy and the worship of the goddess Diana.

Demetrius, a goldsmith, had a thriving business making temples for Diana, the goddess of Ephesus, and through his work earned large wages for his workers. After hearing Paul teach that gods made by human hands are not true gods, he gathered together his workers and all those who practiced the same trade. He spoke to them in these words: "Men, you know that our welfare (wealth) depends on this industry; and you see and hear that, not only in Ephesus but in almost all Asia, this Paul has persuaded and turned aside a crowd of people, saying that gods made with hands are no gods. The danger resulting from this is not only that our industry will fall into disrepute but also that the temple of the great goddess Diana will be held as nothing, and even that the majesty of her who is revered throughout all Asia and throughout the world will be reduced to nothing." He provoked by these words the anger of all those who were gathered with him, who ended by creating chaos and confusion throughout the city.

Chapter 52
Wealth in the Book of 1 Corinthians

1 Corinthians 10:24

24 Let no man seek his own, but every man another's wealth.

Summary

In this verse, the apostle Paul highlights the importance of altruism and consideration for others. He recommends not to seek one's own interest but, rather, to seek the wealth, well-being, joy, or happiness of others.

Part 5 – Wealthy in the Bible

Chapter 53
Wealthy in the Book of Psalms

Psalms 66:8-12 (KJV)

8 O bless our God, ye people, and make the voice of his praise to be heard:

9 Which holdeth our soul in life, and suffereth not our feet to be moved.

10 For thou, O God, hast proved us: thou hast tried us, as silver is tried.

11 Thou broughtest us into the net; thou laidst affliction upon our loins.

12 Thou hast caused men to ride over our heads; we went through fire and through water: but thou broughtest us out into a wealthy place.

Summary

In this text, the psalmist invites everyone to bless God and let the voice of praise be heard in His honor for the life and protection He gives us. He explains how, in order to refine us like silver, God tests us by:

- bringing us into the net
- allowing affliction to be on our loins
- allowing men to ride on our heads
- making us pass through fire and water

The psalmist recognizes that, ultimately, all these trials have led us to a wealthy place.

Chapter 54
Wealthy in the Book of Jeremiah

Jeremiah 49:28-33

28 Against Kedar and against the kingdoms of Hazor, which Nebuchadnezzar king of Babylon shall strike. Thus says the Lord: "Arise, go up to Kedar, And devastate the men of the East!

29 Their tents and their flocks they shall take away. They shall take for themselves their curtains, All their vessels and their camels; And they shall cry out to them, 'Fear is on every side!'

30 "Flee, get far away! Dwell in the depths, O inhabitants of Hazor!" says the Lord. "For Nebuchadnezzar king of Babylon has taken counsel against you, And has conceived a plan against you.

31 "Arise, go up to the wealthy nation that dwells securely," says the Lord, "Which has neither gates nor bars, Dwelling alone.

32 Their camels shall be for booty, And the multitude of their cattle for plunder. I will scatter to all winds those in the farthest corners, And I will bring their calamity from all its sides," says the Lord.

33 "Hazor shall be a dwelling for jackals, a desolation forever; No one shall reside there, Nor son of man dwell in it."

Summary

In this passage, the prophet Jeremiah announces the judgment of God against Kedar and the kingdoms of Hazor by Nebuchadnezzar, king of Babylon.

God instructs Nebuchadnezzar to go up against Kedar and destroy the men of the East. He prophesies that their goods and livestock will be taken away and they will shout out that fear is on every side.

To the inhabitants of the kingdoms of Hazor, God tells them to run and hide deep in caves because King Nebuchadnezzar has taken counsel and made a plan against them. God commands Nebuchadnezzar to go up to this rich and prosperous nation that lives in safety alone, without gates or barriers. He mentions that their camels and their many livestock will go as spoil, the inhabitants will be scattered, including those who are in distant places, and He will bring their calamity on all sides. Furthermore, God mentions that Hazor will be a den of jackals, a desolation forever, and no one will live there.

Conclusion

The theme of wealth in the Bible is both fascinating and multifaceted. Exploring money, prosperity, and wealth in Scripture reveals a deeply nuanced understanding of these concepts, which are not just about material accumulation but are closely tied to spiritual and ethical dimensions.

Money has always played an important role in human life, and the Bible does not fail to reflect this reality. Wealth is presented both as a potential blessing from God and as a spiritual and moral challenge. This duality underscores the importance of approaching wealth with wisdom and a mindset rooted in faith and responsibility.

As believers, we are often faced with making comments and answering questions about wealth and its role in our lives. It is therefore important for us to understand God's intentions on the subject and to rid ourselves of the fear that has been communicated to us by false teachings about wealth for centuries. Speeches such as "Do not cling to earthly goods, bring them to the rectory" have largely contributed to impoverishing the people of God who have abandoned the acquisition of wealth to immoral people, often stupid and empty from within. The current state of moral degradation in our world is the convincing result of these people's inappropriate use of wealth.

Money will never fill the void left inside a person. On the contrary, being an amplifier, money will only accentuate this void. Because, no matter how much money one has, 0 (or emptiness) multiplied by 1 billion will always equal 0 (or emptiness). With this principle, God has made it so that in the process of acquiring wealth, according to the Bible, the Christian becomes wise and mature before arriving there. Because money is so powerful and dangerous, it requires wisdom and spiritual maturity to control and use it in a way that is consistent with God's will and purposes. This call to stewardship is accompanied by a strong emphasis on generosity, especially toward the poor, needy, and marginalized.

The Bible also warns us of the dangers of wealth becoming an object of trust. A balance must be maintained between recognizing the value of wealth and ensuring that it does not become an idol. Wealth should be valued as a gift, not as the ultimate goal or measure of success.

The Bible's teachings on money, prosperity, and wealth provide us with timeless wisdom that is even more relevant today than it was in ancient times. They challenge readers today to critically evaluate their own attitudes toward wealth and to align their financial practices with biblical principles. This involves a commitment to ethical profit, generous giving, responsible management, a constant awareness of the dangers that wealth can pose, and acting wisely at all times.

www.ingramcontent.com/pod-product-compliance
Lightning Source LLC
Chambersburg PA
CBHW011801090426
42811CB00007B/1007